D1232668

# The Landmark Trust Handbook

40th anniversary 1965–2005

**Booking Office telephone**
**01628 825925**
Overseas **+44 1628 825925**

Office  **01628 825920**
Fax  **01628 825417**
Website  **www.landmarktrust.org.uk**
Email  **bookings@landmarktrust.org.uk**

*Left:* Textile design for Dolbelydr by Jennifer Maskell Packer.
Printed by Christian Smith, a trustee of the Landmark Trust
from 1965 until her retirement in 2005.

## Contents

CLARENCE HOUSE

On the eve of the Landmark Trust's fortieth year, I made two contrasting visits to Landmark buildings which, in their different ways, defined for me the inspirational nature and extraordinary range of Landmark's achievements. At Augustus Pugin's house, The Grange in Ramsgate, I saw Landmark at the forefront of building conservation, meeting the people responsible for The Grange's complex and fascinating rebirth: apprentices and craftsmen carrying forward traditional skills of which Pugin himself would have approved; dedicated professionals and Landmark staff; and the partners and generous supporters who had donated the money to make it possible. Two weeks later I was at Dolbelydr in Denbighshire, hearing from a quartet of regular Landmarkers of their uplifting experience staying in this wonderful Tudor manor house rescued from the cusp of total loss by Landmark.

The Landmark Trust is one of those rare organisations that continues to improve with age. Its formula that people staying in Landmarks pay towards their ongoing preservation and maintenance remains as valid as ever, while the flow of further buildings in need of help continues to grow. Over the last forty years it has held to its course, rescuing buildings that would otherwise have been lost and inspiring new generations to experience, learn from and enjoy our heritage. Unobtrusively, it has entered the hearts of tens of thousands of people whose lives have been enriched by staying in or visiting Landmarks.

The Landmark Trust is now an indispensable protector of this country's cultural fabric, a charity admired and respected far beyond these shores and one of which I am inordinately proud to be Patron. I wish it every conceivable success in its utterly vital conservation work.

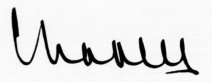

# Introduction

The Ruin, North Yorkshire

# The Landmark Trust

When the first Landmark Trust Handbook was published in 1968, it had 11 pages and featured six newly restored cottages. It was Landmark's first publicity; until then, the fledgling charity had relied upon word of mouth to spread news about its work.

Landmark had been founded in 1965 to prevent the loss or irreversible alteration of small but worthwhile buildings, which were at the time overlooked by the conservation world. It was based on the novel proposition of restoring such buildings and then generating funds for their ongoing and costly maintenance by letting them for holidays, thus guaranteeing their future. Without Landmark's help over the last 40 years, many important buildings would have been lost for ever, buildings with no other use to justify their rescue and support their upkeep.

Landmark usually steps in when all other options have failed, filling a special role in British building conservation. Today in our 40th year, this Handbook features over 180 diverse buildings that you can stay in, a portfolio of national significance, making a unique contribution to the protection of Britain's architectural heritage.

Anyone can stay in a Landmark, enriching their own lives by living for a time in a historic building, while knowing that every holiday spent in a Landmark helps ensure its survival.

## Landmark's Purpose

Landmark's purpose remains the same as it was in 1965: to rescue and restore buildings of historic or architectural interest with their surroundings, and give them new life, a secure future and a contemporary purpose. We strive to ensure that they provide an inspiring and distinctive experience for those who stay in them.

Often we work with others, collaborating as much with national bodies, as with smaller, local ones. Working together brings wider benefit through our work, as with the return of the village green to the community at Peasenhall, or helping to regenerate an urban setting by restoring the Music Room in Lancaster.

Sometimes, our use of part of a building allows us to support its wider use, such as the museum next to the Ancient House in Clare. Several of our buildings came with collections and have museum rooms, or are open to the general public on a regular basis. Lundy Island is a special case, an entire island that we lease from the National Trust and have managed since 1969. Our restoration of its buildings and services has enabled visitors as well as its island community to enjoy a unique place.

As Landmark moves into the twenty-first century, we are also alert to our responsibilities towards the more recent past, apparent in our first post-war building, Anderton House, which opened in 2003.

## Landmark and Education

Education, in its broadest, life-enhancing sense, has always lain at the heart of Landmark, for much can be learnt from living for a while in a historic building. For those who are interested, each Landmark has an album recounting the history of the building and its former inhabitants, as well as its own bookcase of carefully chosen books. An increasing number have their own children's booklet to introduce younger Landmarkers to the building's architecture and history. We also hold Open Days for the general public, with free information available about the building.

*Right:* Landmark often works with other bodies, including the National Trust which owns the Gibside Estate. Restoration of The Banqueting House, Gibside, was completed by Landmark in 1982.

*Below:* The restoration of Wilmington Priory, East Sussex, was completed in 2000, following generous funding from the Heritage Lottery Fund, English Heritage and other Landmark supporters.

*Above right:* Four of Coombe's buildings, including Ford Cottage, featured in Landmark's first Handbook, having been acquired to help preserve the hamlet's special qualities.

## Landmark and Funding

Conservation, as it is now called, was in its infancy in 1965 and the wider context in which Landmark operates has changed significantly since then. Statutory protection of listed buildings has been strengthened and since 1994 the Heritage Lottery Fund has provided a much-needed injection of funds into conserving historic buildings.

Landmark's core funding for its projects has also changed. We have come of age and, after over three decades of unstintingly generous support from the Manifold Trust, we now rely on the generosity of a much broader range of supporters.

Lack of financial viability is typically the chief cause of the distress of the buildings we take on. While the eventual letting income will pay for their ongoing maintenance, we fundraise for the restoration, and sometimes acquisition, of each building we accept into our care.

We often receive generous support from the Heritage Lottery Fund and statutory grant-givers for a proportion of the acquisition and restoration costs, but we must find the balance elsewhere through wider fundraising campaigns. Individual supporters and charitable trusts are vital to our work, because, as our first six cottages demonstrate, we have always believed that the unremarkable past has as much value as the grand, a belief with which statutory funding is increasingly unable to help. In celebrating 40 years of rescuing buildings, we thank everyone who has helped make this possible and shares our passion for giving historic buildings new life.

## Landmark Outside the UK

Landmark has four buildings in Italy and four in America, the latter through an independent sister charity, Landmark Trust USA. All these buildings have a cultural connection with Britain, whether as Rudyard Kipling's house in Naulakha or as the Brownings' house, Casa Guidi in Florence. The Italian buildings, which include a Palladian villa, are a source of enormous pride to us, although their acquisition belongs to the time when independent means allowed us to pursue such dreams outside the UK funding structure. Even now, the flexibility of our approach would not prevent us extending once more beyond our shores, if the right set of circumstances presented themselves.

## A Unique Contribution

In numerous ways, large and small, over the past 40 years Landmark has helped prevent the erosion of the past by unthinking modern development or neglect. Banqueting houses, towers, forts, follies, castles and cottages have been saved which otherwise would have been lost. Through their careful restoration, Landmark has built up a national reputation in which we take pride and which we strive to maintain.

Above all, Landmarks continue to provide people with the opportunity to live in historic buildings, an experience altogether different from that which the day visitor can glean. In helping to communicate and celebrate the richness and relevance of the past, we aim to reinforce the notion that, perhaps more than ever in this modern world, the past remains part of the warp and weft of us all, and is to be cherished.

# The Landmark Trust 1965–2005

The Landmark Trust was founded in 1965 as a building conservation charity to preserve small buildings or sites of historic interest or architectural merit.

## 1966

Church Cottage, an early Victorian slate cottage in Cardiganshire, is the first building acquired by the Landmark Trust. It remains a popular Landmark, although the church after which it was named was demolished in 2000.

## 1969

Lundy is leased from the National Trust and Landmark sets out to restore and run the island. Improving services and its buildings gradually, Lundy now has 23 Landmarks.

## 1987

Crownhill Fort, an extensive Victorian fort built to protect Plymouth's naval base, is acquired. Not only is a Landmark created but the extensive grounds, tunnels, weaponry and buildings are restored. It is currently the only Landmark licensed for civil weddings.

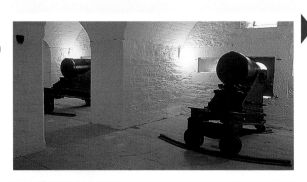

## 1973

The Pineapple, an elaborate summerhouse, is leased from the National Trust for Scotland. It is the first and still the most photographed of our 18 Scottish Landmarks.

## 1981

The first London Landmark is restored, 45a Cloth Fair. No. 43, long the home of Sir John Betjeman, later also becomes a Landmark. The addition of Princelet Street in 2004, means there are now three central London Landmarks.

## 1978

The Saddell Estate, Kintyre, one of Landmark's best loved landscapes, is taken on. The restoration of Saddell House as a Landmark in 2004 marked the completion of Saddell's six buildings and a 26-year vision.

## 1990

In Landmark's silver jubilee year, a record-breaking 10 restorations are completed including Kingswear Castle, the East Banqueting House and Frenchman's Creek.

## 2005

The Ruin, a small pavilion perched above a steep wooded gorge opens as the 181st Landmark. This was one of the longest projects in our 40-year history, having been first brought to Landmark's attention in 1989.

## 1993

Having established Landmark Trust USA as a sister charity, in 1991, Naulakha, Rudyard Kipling's Vermont home, opens as the first US Landmark. Kipling wrote *The Jungle Books* in the study.

## 2004

Restoration begins of Augustus Pugin's family home, The Grange, Ramsgate. It is due to open as a Landmark in early 2006. Acquired in 1997, this is Landmark's most expensive restoration to date.

## 1994

Years of neglect meant extensive restoration was needed before the Villa Saraceno, designed by Palladio in the sixteenth century, could open as Landmark's largest building to date – sleeping 16. An important and unexpected discovery was its frescoes, lying beneath layers of limewash.

## 2001

The restoration of Auchinleck House, a fine eighteenth century Scottish country villa and former home of James Boswell, is completed.

## 1997

Goddards, one of Edwin Lutyens' most important early houses, becomes a Landmark. The Lutyens Trust, having found its care too costly, leased it to Landmark. They continue to retain use of the Library.

# Rescuing Buildings

### A Continuing Need

When Landmark was founded in 1965, the concept that smaller historic buildings were worth preserving was barely developed and the framework of protection and funding for historic buildings that we take for granted today did not exist. By 2005, while much has changed, the flow of buildings in need of rescue and a secure future is as constant as ever, making Landmark's role just as necessary today.

### What Makes a Landmark?

We receive on average three approaches a week about potential Landmarks; many are for sale on the open market or not at risk and so are unsuitable. Yet some – suggested by Landmark supporters or members of the public, local authorities, private estates or other charities, or spotted by us – deserve further investigation. We look for buildings that are in some sense at risk and significant, whether architecturally, historically or culturally, and which would make a rewarding place to stay.

The decision whether to take on a building is made by Landmark's Trustees. An evaluation study follows and then acquisition details are finalised. Even then a project may stumble: access arrangements may come to nothing or the owners may change their mind, and then the building will be filed away in our archives (often to surface again, still in distress, years later). Projects that proceed are therefore only the tip of the iceberg of the many we are always working on behind the scenes.

### Preliminaries

Once acquisition is complete, Landmark shifts into higher gear. We prefer to commission our architects according to region and their familiarity with the needs of old buildings and the fragility of their patina. Often the project architects have worked with us before, but their ingenuity will always be tested, especially in buildings never intended for habitation, and where kitchens and bathrooms must be inserted where, until now, there was no water or electricity.

A building analyst reports on the building's fabric and documents are researched to inform the final scheme. Careful record photography is commissioned prior to restoration to help with the scheme and for archival purposes.

Our restoration is guided by certain principles. We prefer to repair rather than renew and will respect alterations and additions that have become a part of a building's personality. However, we are prepared to consider reversing past change: perhaps inferior work obscures a finer original, or decay has progressed so far that reinstatement would be conjectural or financially unjustifiable. Rather than commit to unseemly alteration, we trust to our visitors' sense of adventure and ask them to adapt to the building rather than the reverse. This respect extends to the fabric of outbuildings or ruins in the grounds: to these

*Above:* Piecing together Dolbelydr's internal timber frame.

*Below left:* Reassembling the plaster frieze at the West Banqueting House, Old Campden House.

# Dolbelydr

Dolbelydr's architectural significance as a largely unaltered, late-Tudor manor house had long been recognised in the lists and registers of such things. Yet it was a roofless ruin when it first came to Landmark's attention in 1982, locked within farmland in Denbighshire with no access and no prospect of rescue.

We could not help then, but our archives have a purpose and we are persistent in our pursuit of worthwhile buildings. We revived discussions in the mid-1990s and finally, in 1999, the Dorothy Stroud Bequest enabled us to buy both ruin and access. Emergency scaffolding was put up immediately, but it took two more years to raise the funds for restoration.

Restoration involves great intimacy with the building, especially when it requires such careful sifting and reconstruction. Roof timbers lay where they had fallen, while the

newel post from the staircase was returned to us by a caring local resident. Skilled craftsmen with an intimate knowledge of traditional building materials were also required. This intimacy lingers for those staying in the building, who can also share quiet satisfaction in the honesty of new oak against the patina of old, the gentle variation of lime plaster over hand-riven laths and the ripple of greenish glass, sourced to match a single surviving original piece.

**Above:** *Landmark's rescue of Dolbelydr was completed in 2003, following generous funding from donors including the Heritage Lottery Fund, Cadw, the Welsh Development Agency, the Esmeé Fairbairn Foundation and the Welsh Tourist Board.*

**Left:** *Unlived in since 1912, Dolbelydr was very overgrown with vegetation. Careful examination of the accumulated site rubble, meant many original materials were recovered which could be used in restoring Dolbelydr.*

we will usually do as little as possible, keeping them safe to be explored and to awaken the memory of an earlier landscape.

We often need help from specialists, such as steeplejacks, engineers or archaeologists. Listed building consent must be obtained, and water, electricity and drainage arrangements agreed. Finally, a quantity surveyor draws up a specification for the work needed and contractors' estimates are obtained.

### Funding Landmark's Work

Meanwhile, and crucially, Landmark's fundraising team has also been busy – work cannot begin until

we have raised the money for the restoration. Where possible a Heritage Lottery Fund application is drawn up, and funding sought from English Heritage, Cadw or Historic Scotland. An appeal directly to Landmark supporters or applications to charitable trusts may be made. Perhaps a more lateral funding approach is possible, through area regeneration grants, the local authority, or a generous private donor with a passion for the building, its architect or someone who lived there. Legacies are also increasingly important in funding Landmark projects. No two funding packages are ever the same and sometimes they take years to assemble – but we are used to taking a long view.

## The Ruin

In the 1750s and 60s William Aislabie created a picturesque landscape at Hackfall, North Yorkshire, once as famous as Aislabie's other garden at nearby Studley Royal. The climax to its tour was the double-fronted banqueting house on Mowbray Point, known as The Ruin.

It was truly a ruin when first brought to our attention in 1989 by the then newly formed Hackfall Trust, whose aim is to restore the gardens. Collaboration with other like-minded bodies has always been part of our mission, although here it took another 12 years before lease and funding arrangements were complete. It is often harder to raise money to restore a small building like this, and, after grants from English Heritage, Harrogate District Council and The Monument Trust, patience was needed to assemble the remaining funds from private sources, including an appeal to Landmark supporters.

Repairing the stonework was a particular challenge, to keep some sense of the erosion caused by the Yorkshire weather and of precariously poised keystones in the 'ruinous' elevation, while also consolidating and rebuilding its domes and oculi. Inside, the joinery and plasterwork in the polite central chamber are once more crisp and intact, incorporating salvaged remnants.

**Top:** *The method of construction used to repair The Ruin's mock Roman arches is little changed from when it was first built, with wooden frames forming the arches, the stones then being bedded in lime mortar.*

**Right:** *The walls in the central room are painted a vivid blue verditer, a pigment found by paint analysis to have been used by Mr Aislabie.*

## The Restoration Process

Finally, with everything in place, the contractors can move on site and there is noise and cheerful bustle where before there was silence and slow decay. We rely on the perseverance and uncompromising standards of our contractors and craftsmen, who are local wherever possible, helping to ensure the survival of distinctive regional techniques. Knowing that we are able to support and encourage craft skills that may otherwise struggle to survive is no small part of the satisfaction in the overall restoration process. There is good reason to keep faith with these traditional building materials and skills. They ensure honest repair and, just as importantly, they allow an old building quite literally to breathe and remain in healthy equilibrium with its environment.

Even a specialist contractor is unlikely to carry all the crafts needed to restore a building, especially for fine finishes. Conservators of paint or papier mâché, plasterers skilled in replacing cornices and mouldings, joiners who can transform planks into panelling may all be called upon.

*Left:* A stonemason working at Auchinleck House, Ayrshire.

### Furnishing

Once the contractor moves out, the building catches its breath before Landmark's furnishing team moves in. Paint colours and curtains have already been chosen, often informed by physical and documentary research. Kitchen and other modern equipment is selected, together with books that will help appreciation of the building.

In our furniture workshops, furniture and pictures that evoke the building's mood and history have been brought together, being repaired and re-polished or sometimes specially made by our joiners. Now, in a last flurry of activity, vanloads of furniture arrive at the building. There are always logistics to overcome:

beds may be winched in through trapdoors, last minute adjustments made to take account of walls or floors that may not quite be true, larger pieces even dismantled and reassembled in situ – but here at last the final alchemy is worked.

The vans depart and the building is silent once again, but now it is an expectant silence as the rooms glow with new-found life and purpose. Infused with quiet sunlight filtering through glass, beautiful in its small imperfections, a smell of beeswax rising from ancient boards, the building waits for the key to turn in the lock and the first Landmarkers to arrive to launch it into the next phase of its history. The process of creating a Landmark is complete.

## The Grange

The Grange in Ramsgate was built by Augustus Pugin for himself and his family in the 1840s. Despite its Grade I status, it fell into neglect and decline. There was permission to convert it into flats when it came onto the market in 1997, but no other body was willing to rescue the house from this inappropriate development while still able to ensure public access and a secure future. With a generous grant from the Heritage Lottery Fund, we were able to make a rare purchase on the open market.

After painstaking research, we found that the evidence was best for the building as it

was left by Augustus Pugin. Our belief that the house should therefore be returned to an appearance that he would recognise, while at the same time functioning successfully as a Landmark, involved long and patient negotiation with interested bodies.

In parallel, we had to fundraise for our most expensive project to date, for the glory of The Grange lies as much in its rich decorative finishes as its structure. Its completion will form a fitting climax to our 40th anniversary, a clear example of Landmark's broadening role within British conservation.

**Below left:** *Paint conservators have prepared test panels on The Grange's painted ceilings and friezes to allow us to approve the restoration methodology.*

**Below:** *With support from the Heritage Lottery Fund, English Heritage, Thanet District Council, private trusts and many private individuals, the project team, including apprentice craftsmen, finally went on site in 2004.*

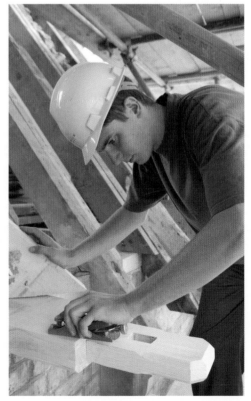

Beamsley Hospital, North Yorkshire

# Landmark Holidays

All the Landmarks shown in this Handbook can be rented by anyone, at all times of the year, for periods ranging from a weekend to three weeks. The Handbook and a Price List are all you need. Each building is illustrated and described, telling something of its story. There are maps suggesting places of interest in the area and plans showing how the accommodation is arranged, particularly with regard to beds.

## Landmarks

Each has been chosen because it is remarkable in some way, because it needed our help and because we believe people will enjoy staying in it. Some were not designed to be lived in and the living arrangements can be unusual as a result. We aim as far as possible to preserve them in the form in which they were built, adapting them for modern use only in minor ways, but nevertheless seeking a high standard of comfort.

## Furniture and Furnishings

We like our buildings to feel comfortably lived-in and not as if they were decorated and furnished yesterday.

Our furniture is chosen to fit in happily with its surroundings. Most of it is old, simple and good, with the occasional unexpected flourish. The rugs and carpets have generally seen enough use elsewhere to make them agreeable to the eye, but many of the curtains are specially designed and printed for each Landmark. The pictures usually have a special reason for being there. Indeed it is our aim to preserve and restore not only the buildings but also the outlook on life which created them.

## Local Information

Each Landmark building has its own History Album: a careful account of its past and our restoration of its fabric. We also provide each one with those books that we think our visitors would like to find there – books about the neighbourhood and works of literature with local associations. There are also jigsaw puzzles, large

*Below:* Sackville House, West Sussex.

*Below right:* Old Place of Monreith, Dumfries and Galloway.

scale maps marking footpaths and a logbook in which visitors can write their own discoveries for the benefit of their successors.

### Facilities

At a practical level, all buildings have modern bathrooms and kitchens and plenty of kitchen equipment. There is enough crockery and cutlery to entertain two extra people for dinner. Some Landmarks have dishwashers, washing machines and freezers too. Apart from this, we try to keep intrusive equipment to a minimum and do not provide televisions or telephones. Details of the equipment in each Landmark can be found in the Price List. All beds, however ancient or exotic the head and foot, have modern mattresses, blankets and pillows. We also provide towels and linen. A baby's cot is normally available but bedding is not provided.

Every building has heating of some kind, and where possible there is an open fire or stove as well. We do not provide logs or coal, but neither do we charge extra for gas or electricity. You may wish to bring extra jerseys and hot-water bottles for some buildings, as indicated in the information supplied on booking.

### Access

Many Landmarks can be reached by public transport. If you do go by car, you will find that in one or two places you must park it at some distance from the building.

### Gardens

We own enough land with most of our buildings to give you somewhere to sit outside and a few have substantial gardens. Even in towns or villages there is often a terrace or a flat roof. Sometimes we own the surrounding fields. These are usually let for grazing, but you are free to walk or play in them. Gardens described as enclosed will not necessarily restrain adventurous children or dogs. Well-behaved dogs are welcome, except where the problems or temptations are too great.

### Housekeepers

Every Landmark has a Housekeeper, who will make it ready for you. Some of them knew the building before we did, or have cared for it as long as we have. They can be invisible if you wish, but many become friends, and talking to them and getting to know them is part of the pleasure of the holiday, as the logbooks testify.

*Below left:* Crownhill Fort, Devon.

*Below:* Robin Hood's Hut, Somerset.

*Above:* Methwold Old Vicarage, Norfolk.

*Bottom:* Saddell House, Argyll and Bute.

## Booking a Landmark

Landmarks may be booked by the week or for shorter stays. Each property is described in the Handbook, with additional information and prices shown in the Price List. When you are ready to book, please call our Booking Office whose staff will check availability, make recommendations and confirm your holiday plans.

There may be more that you would like to ask about spending a holiday in a Landmark. If so, our Booking Office has, or can quickly find out, the answers to your questions.

Changes do take place and it is essential to use the current Landmark Trust Handbook and Price List, which includes our booking conditions and much else you need to know. Availability is updated daily on our website or you may call the Booking Office.

The Booking Office is open:
Monday to Friday 9am–6pm
Saturday 10am–4pm
It is closed on Sundays and Bank Holidays.

**Please contact our Booking Office**
## 01628 825925
Overseas **+44 1628 825925**

Office **01628 825920**
Fax **01628 825417**
Website **www.landmarktrust.org.uk**
Email **bookings@landmarktrust.org.uk**

The Mackintosh Building

Perth

Gargunnock House

Stirling

The Hill House          The Pineapple

Edinburgh

Wemyss Bay

Ascog                   Roslin

SCOTLAND

Saddell
Tangy Mill
Campbeltown            Auchinleck House

Stranraer              Castle of Park       Brinkburn Mill
                                            Morpeth Castle
                                            Newcastle-
                       Old Place of Monreith    upon-Tyne
                       Coop House   Causeway House
                                    Carlisle  The Banqueting House

                                            Durham

                       The Grammar School
                       Howthwaite          Richmond    Whitby
                                    Culloden Tower            The Pigsty

                                    Kendal

                                            The Ruin

                       Lancaster
                       The Music Room    Skipton    York
                                    Beamsley Hospital
                       Calverley Old Hall   Leeds    Cawood Castle

                                    Manchester
                       Liverpool    Edale Mill   Sheffield    The Château
                                                              Lincoln

                       Conwy                      Matlock
Caernarfon    Dolbelydr
Bath Tower                Wrexham
              Rhiwddolion         North Street
                                    Nottingham
                       Plas Uchaf            Derby    Grantham   Appleton   Houghton
                       St Winifred's Well   Alton Station        Water Tower   West Lodge
                       Ingestre Pavilion  Tixall   Swarkestone Pavilion   The House
                       Stafford   Gatehouse   Knowle Hill       of Correction
                       Shrewsbury   Iron Bridge House           King's Lynn        Norwich
                       Poultry Cottage            Leicester   Peterborough   Methwold
                                    Langley Gatehouse                        Old Vicarage
                       Montgomery   The White House                                Manor Farm
                                    Bromfield Priory   Birmingham   ENGLAND        New Inn
                       WALES        Gatehouse        Northampton   Lynch Lodge   Bury St Edmunds
                                    Ludlow   Lock Cottage   Bedford              Aldeburgh
                                                        Cambridge   Purton Green   Ipswich   Martello Tower
                       Stockwell Farm          Worcester   Stratford-   The Bath          The Ancient House   Freston Tower
                       Cardigan              upon-Avon   House                   Colchester
                       Maesyronen Chapel   Shelwick Court            The Tower,   Warden Abbey   Peake's House
                       Church Cottage        Hereford   Old Campden House   Canons Ashby
                                    Brecon                        Tewkesbury   Gothic Temple
St David's                                    Abbey Gatehouse   Buckingham
Tower Hill             Paxton's Tower Lodge   St Mary's Lane
                       Carmarthen            Gloucester   Oxford   The Steward's House   Cloth Fair
West Blockhouse        Clytha Castle   Field House            The Old Parsonage   Princelet Street
              Pembroke                   Cirencester                         Prospect Tower
              Monkton Old Hall                               Hampton    London          The Grange
                                                             Court
                       Cardiff   Bristol                     Palace
                                                        Goddards   Obriss Farm   Maidstone   Dover
                       Woodspring Priory      Bath
                                    Beckford's Tower               Hole Cottage
                                    Elton House
              Lundy    Anderton House   Marshal Wade's House   East Grinstead
                       Stogursey Castle   Parish   Wells              Sackville House
                       Gurney Manor   House   The Old Hall
                       Bideford       Robin Hood's Hut   Salisbury   Southampton   Lewes   Laughton Place
Peppercombe    The Library              Taunton           The Wardrobe   Luttrell's      Wilmington Priory
Coombe         South Street   The Priest's House         Tower   Chichester
                                    Shute Gatehouse   Fox Hall
                       Exeter   Wolveton   Woodsford
The College    Wortham Manor   Gatehouse   Castle
Launceston            Margells   Dorchester
                       Lettaford   Peters Tower
                       Endsleigh
Whiteford Temple   Danescombe Mine
              Plymouth   Crownhill   Kingswear Castle
Lower                      Fort
Porthmeor   Truro
Penzance
The Egyptian      Frenchman's Creek
House

Channel Islands        Alderney
                       Fort
                       Clonque

Guernsey

Sark

Jersey    Nicolle Tower

0                    miles                    100

# Landmarks by size

UK Landmarks

Martello Tower, Suffolk

# Abbey Gatehouse

For up to 2 people
Solid fuel stove

Parking nearby
Steep staircases

Tewkesbury is an exceptional town. The abbey church alone is worth making the journey for. Along the main street and in the narrow lanes running off it, medieval and Tudor buildings blend pleasantly with those of later centuries.

Abbey Gatehouse, which we lease from the trust that guards the surroundings of the abbey, is a grand building of about 1500, restored in 1849 by J. Medland. His work was thorough but skilful – indeed it is difficult to tell now just how much of the stonework he renewed. The gatehouse has only one room, a very fine one on the first floor. At one end of this we have built a gallery, rather like an organ case. Inside there is everything you need but do not want to see and on its top you sleep, close under the moulded beams of the roof, painted the same colours as the vault of the abbey choir. The soaring west window of the abbey rises only a few yards from your door, as you dwell in the 'lodging over the great gate'.

## From the logbook

*Wonderful to wake up in the morning with the sunlight illuminating the angel corbel.*

*Being a lapsed choirboy, I found the Evensong Service very moving.*

*The best things for us were the absolute peace, privacy and the Abbey Church itself.*

*A magical, lovely and romantic place. A thoroughly memorable time.*

Gallery level

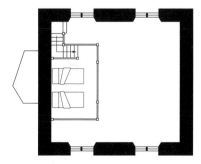

First floor

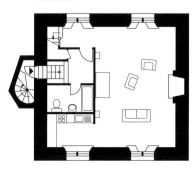

# Alton Station

Alton, Staffordshire

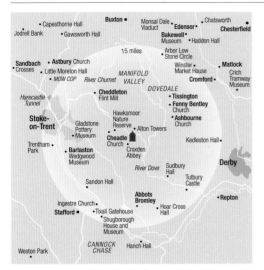

For up to 6 people
Parking nearby

Steep staircase
Dogs allowed

This is the only Italianate railway station in Staffordshire, a notable example of a vanishing class of building. We were indeed grateful to the County Council for conveying it to us in 1970. The railway has gone; but in its heyday the platforms took 12-coach excursion trains from the Potteries.

Its architect was probably H. A. Hunt, an architect-engineer who designed other stations on this line, which opened in 1849. Built by the North Staffordshire Railway (the 'Knotty') to a befitting standard for the Earl of Shrewsbury, then owner of Alton Towers, it stands in marvellous surroundings, both beautiful and interesting. Pugin's Alton Castle rises out of the trees across the valley of the Churnet, like something from the Carinthia of Dornford Yates, and Alton Towers itself, with its famous garden, lies immediately behind.

During our work on the house a disused flue was found to have been blocked with porters' waistcoats; and the plumbing we installed produced at first a strange chuffing sound – doubtless the yearning of this house for the sound and smell of great engines wreathed in steam.

From the logbook
*The only trouble with this place is that time goes too fast.*

Ground floor

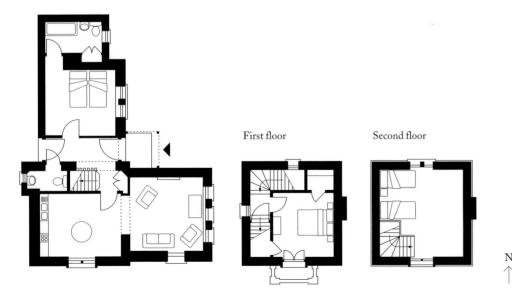

First floor

Second floor

N

# The Ancient House

Clare, Suffolk

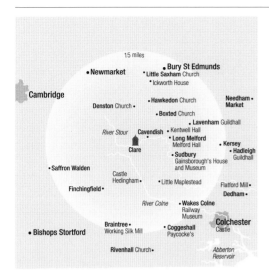

For up to 2 people
Open fire
Small enclosed
garden

Parking on street
Steep staircase
Sloping floors
Dogs allowed

Standing at the south-west corner of St Peter and St Paul's churchyard, the Ancient House is a picturesque medieval timber-framed building in this remarkably unspoilt market town. Its elaborate pargeting (raised plaster decoration), so distinctive a form of vernacular decoration in East Anglia, bears the date '1473', and is one of the most celebrated examples of this art in the country. Alec Clifton-Taylor, in *The Pattern of English Building*, mentions watching two elderly pargeters working on repairs there with a compound of lime and sand, horsehair and horse fat. The House incorporates a handsome moulded timber ceiling in the ground floor chamber and elaborately carved oriel windows there and in the first floor bedroom. Staying here you will have an enviable close-up view of the great wool church.

A local farmer, Charles W. Byford, acquired the Ancient House in the early 1930s to prevent its removal to the United States and it was subsequently given to Clare Parish Council. The Council invited us to create a Landmark here while they maintain a museum in half of the building, thus together safeguarding the future of the house. Close by is Clare Priory, founded for the Austin Friars in 1248, the earliest house of the order in England, and The Cliftons, a building whose exuberant sixteenth century brick chimneys are richly decorated with circular shafts, Tudor patterns and star tops. Beyond there is a wealth of little-changed Suffolk villages to discover, with some of the country's finest Tudor brickwork.

From the logbook
*It never ceases to amaze me that feeling you get when you walk into a Landmark for the first time – is this all for me?*

Ground floor

First floor

$\rightarrow$ z

# Anderton House

Goodleigh, Devon

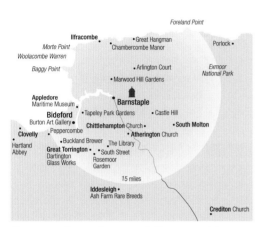

For up to 5 people
Enclosed garden

Adjacent parking
Dogs allowed

Buildings of any age can find themselves at risk. As a building designed by a living architect, Anderton House was a new departure for us when we acquired it in 2000. We chose it for all the reasons we usually apply to older buildings. For all its modernity, Anderton House is as much at home in the rolling Devon landscape it overlooks as the longhouses which inspired its profile. It is an exceptional example of uncompromisingly modern design executed in simple materials, happily caught before changing tastes had been allowed to blur its clean lines or site drainage problems to damage its fabric. It is listed Grade II*.

The Anderton family commissioned the house from Peter Aldington in 1969. It is instantly evocative of those days, with a nod to Frank Lloyd Wright in the functional treatment of the bedrooms and for Peter Aldington, 'perhaps the nearest we came to an integration of inside and outside spaces', the ultimate aim of pioneer modern architects.

The roof appears to float cleverly over the spacious open plan living area with its sliding glass walls. The house retains all its contemporary materials and detailing and is furnished to match. Here is a comfortable family home lifted to a different level of experience by the mind of an architect who is a master of his chosen idiom. Revisiting this more recent past is to be highly recommended.

From the logbook
*The illusion of being outside when in never ceases to amaze.*

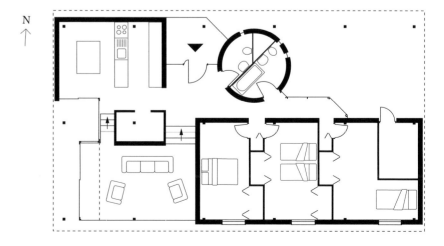

# Appleton Water Tower

Sandringham, Norfolk

For up to 4 people
Open fire
Enclosed garden

Adjacent parking
Steep staircase
Dogs allowed

A public-spirited local landowner gave us a lease of this exceptional Victorian tower. There is seldom an opportunity to preserve a functional building such as this, let alone one of such quality.

It was designed by Robert Rawlinson and the foundation stone was laid in July 1877 by the Princess of Wales. On the ground and first floor was a dwelling for the custodian, with a viewing room above reached by an outside stair. The flues from all the fireplaces passed through the centre of the iron tank to prevent the water from freezing – a typically Victorian idea, original, simple and practical.

From the terrace on top of the tank, which is protected by an ornate cast-iron railing, and from the room below, there is a view on all sides over miles of wide, open landscape. Here, on this exposed hilltop, you can even see a distant gleam of the Wash.

From the logbook
*A toad guards the steps by the side gate and the garden is alive with wild animals and birds: we saw a deer on the lawn one evening.*

*Much time was spent on top viewing the countryside through binoculars, watching the sun set and looking at the stars on clear nights.*

*Time a walk from Stiffkey to ensure you miss the incoming tide and you can go 3 miles towards Blakeney Point. We got within 51 yards of the seals without scaring them off.*

*Squeals of excitement as we explored the Tower.*

There is a bathroom
on the third floor.

Second floor

N
↑

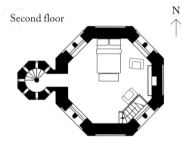

First floor

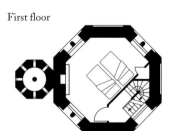

Ground floor

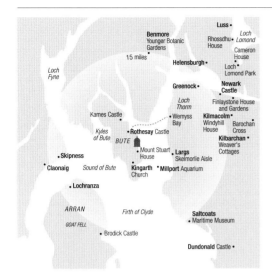

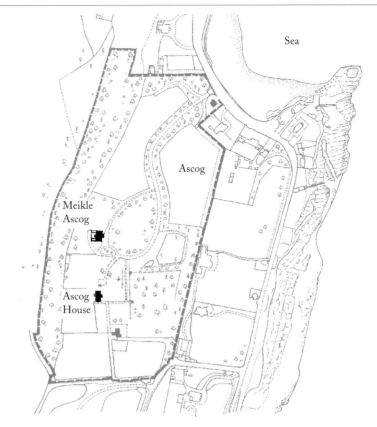

Two houses, one for 9 and one for 10.

Bute has been called the Scottish Isle of Wight, and certainly Rothesay, its capital, with its Winter Garden and decorative ironwork, is reminiscent of the South Coast.

Ascog lies on the sheltered east coast of the island. Trees (especially beech) and shrubs (Charles Rennie Mackintosh drew fuchsias here) grow lushly in its mild climate. It has been gently developed as a superior resort since the 1840s, with a scattering of respectable houses above the bay. Building on the shoreline was wisely forbidden.

One such house stands in the large and secluded grounds of the old mansion house of Ascog, once home to a branch of the Stewarts. We have acquired both buildings, which stand a few hundred yards apart, each looking over its own, rather different, garden.

Ascog House is a typical laird's house of the seventeenth century, with projecting stair turret, dormer windows and crow-stepped gables. When we bought it, it was nearly, but not completely, engulfed by clumsy Victorian additions. These we removed, to restore its true proportions and dignified character. An impressive and soundly built Edwardian stair tower, on the other hand, we kept as a free-standing structure, into which we fitted an extra bedroom and bathroom.

There are frequent ferries from Wemyss Bay, less than an hour from Glasgow.

From the logbook
*Loved everything – especially the swings, snowdrops, the moonlit sea, mountains and palm trees.*

*We have walked, cycled, golfed and lazed around – wonderful.*

*Our favourite walk was Stravannan Bay – we had it completely to ourselves!*

# Ascog

## Ascog House

Seen from the front, the house's main rooms are on the first floor, reached by a wide turn-pike stair. Go round behind and the rise of the ground brings them level with the garden. Inside, the arrangement of the rooms is new but there are old fireplaces, including in the kitchen a noble fragment of a magnificent carved chimney piece from an early stage in the building's history.

Most of the windows were enlarged in the usual fashion of the eighteenth century, set in deep embrasures. Those on the west look out over the old kitchen garden to the wooded hill behind, while those on the east overlook the rediscovered paths and terraces of a late Victorian formal garden, thought to have been designed by Edward Latrobe-Bateman. The best view of all is from the cap house, the tiny perfect bedroom in the top of the stair turret.

For up to 9 people
Open fire
Large garden
Adjacent parking
Spiral staircase
Dogs allowed

Turret room

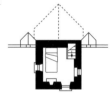

Second floor

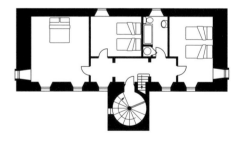

First floor

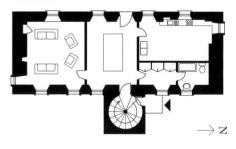

→ N

There is another twin bedroom and bathroom in Tom's Tower, 20 feet from the main house and seen on the right in the top photograph.

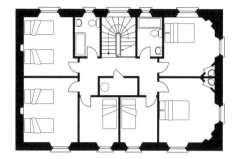
First floor

Ground floor

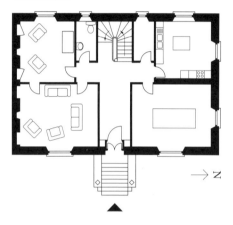

→ z

## Meikle Ascog

Meikle Ascog is what nineteenth century guide books called a neat villa. Its builder, and possibly designer, was an engineer called Robert Thom, who bought the property in 1830. Thom's greatest achievement (besides the sensitive development of Ascog) was to succeed, where engineers such as Watt and Rennie had failed, in the quest to provide Greenock with water – the loch from which it comes is named after him.

In its arrangement, his house reflects a logical and inventive personality, being laid out in the most rational way possible to achieve the most agreeable result: every room is pleasant to be in. The windows look out over a shrubbery, with the sea and the mainland beyond, framed by fine trees. Low sills in the drawing-room and dining-room ensure that this view can be enjoyed, even when sitting down.

For up to 10 people
Open fire
Large garden
Adjacent parking
Dogs allowed

# Auchinleck House

Ochiltree, Ayrshire

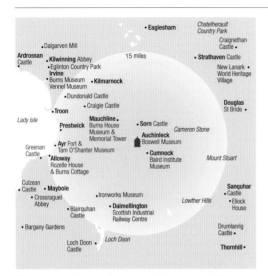

For up to 13 people
Open fire
Open grounds

Adjacent parking
Dogs allowed

Perhaps the finest example of an eighteenth century country villa to survive in Scotland, Auchinleck House is where the renowned biographer James Boswell indulged his penchant for 'old laird and family ideas'. Built around 1760 by Boswell's father Lord Auchinleck, its architect is unknown; it seems likely that Lord Auchinleck himself had a hand in the neo-Classical design, perhaps influenced by the Adam brothers. Boswell's friend and mentor Dr. Samuel Johnson famously argued over politics with Lord Auchinleck in the library here, when they visited at the end of their tour of the Hebrides in 1773. Once inherited by Boswell, the house was host to much 'social glee', which he recorded in his Book of Company and Liquors.

Auchinleck House itself expresses the rich spirit of the Scottish Enlightenment, combining Classical purity in the main elevation with a baroque exuberance in the pavilions and the elaborately carved pediment. We have restored not only the house with its magnificent library looking across to Arran, but also the pavilions, the obelisks and the great bridge across the Dippol Burn, on whose picturesque banks are an ice-house and grotto.

Visitors to the house pass beneath an extract, chosen from Horace by Lord Auchinleck, carved into the pediment: *Quod petis, hic est, Est Ulubris, animus si te non deficit aequus* ('Whatever you seek is here, in this remote place, if only you have a good firm mind'). We are sure this will speak as clearly to those who stay at Auchinleck today as it did to James Boswell himself.

From the logbook
*The house swallowed the children – just occasional sightings.*

*We recommend Scrabble using the Samuel Johnson dictionary only.*

*Parts of the ground floor are open to the public by appointment only on Wednesday afternoons, from the Wednesday after Easter until October. The grounds will be open throughout the spring and summer.*

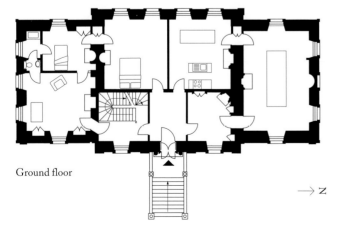

Ground floor

First floor

→ N

There is a further bathroom and also a cloakroom with WC in the basement.

# The Banqueting House

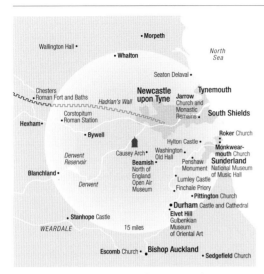

For up to 4 people        Shower only
Solid fuel stove          Dogs allowed
Adjacent parking

Gibside was inherited in 1722 by George Bowes, a landowner and public figure made rich by coal. After his first wife died, he made Gibside his home and set about embellishing the park. The Banqueting House seems to have been finished by 1746. It was designed by Daniel Garrett, a former assistant of Lord Burlington's to stand in the highest part of the park, looking over the Derwent valley.

When we first saw The Banqueting House in 1977 it was almost entirely roofless and the porch and crocketed gables had collapsed. The park, now happily transferred to the National Trust by the Earl of Strathmore and open to the public, was let to the Forestry Commission and The Banqueting House was hidden by trees.

Here was, however, an important building of most original design, part of a famous landscape. The Forestry Commission agreed to give up their lease of it and the Strathmore

Estate then sold us the freehold. Most of the missing stonework was found nearby and inside we were able to save much of the plasterwork and joinery of one room. But the Great Room was just a shell: here we replaced only the main elements of Garrett's design, known from an old photograph.

The Banqueting House now stands in a grassy clearing, looking down to an octagonal pool and the valley beyond. Nearby, the Column of British Liberty rises high above the trees and a little further off lies the Gibside chapel, designed by James Paine in 1760 to hold the remains of George Bowes, ancestor of our Queen.

From the logbook
*We imagined we had mastered the art of seeing through the understatements in the Handbook description. Wrong again. The Banqueting House easily exceeded all expectations.*

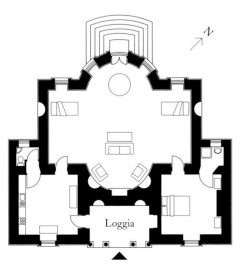

Loggia

# The Bath House

Near Stratford-upon-Avon, Warwickshire

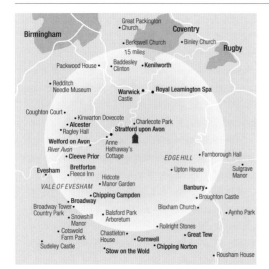

The benefits of a cold bath were held to be almost limitless by medical opinion of the eighteenth century and many country houses were equipped with one. The Bath House here, it is thought, was designed in 1748 by the gentleman-architect Sanderson Miller for his friend Sir Charles Mordaunt. Good historical fun was had by all: the rough masonry of Antiquity, used for the bath chamber, is contrasted with the polished smoothness of the new Augustan age seen in the room above, where the bathers recovered.

Even in the upper room there is a hint of the subterranean, with a dome hung with coolly dripping icicles. Here the walls have also been frosted with shells, arranged in festoons as if 'by some invisible sea-nymph or triton for their private amusement'. This was the idea of Mrs Delany, better known for her flower pictures, who advised the Mordaunt daughters on where to find the shells. Their work was skilfully reproduced by Diana Reynell, after terrible damage by vandals.

The Bath House, at the end of a long and gated drive, has one main room to live in, but in its deep woodland setting, so near to the Forest of Arden, 'you may fleet the time carelessly, as they did in the golden world'.

From the logbook
*It's possible to wake up and think one's a mermaid.*

*This must be the poshest bedsit in Warwickshire.*

For up to 2 people
Open fire

Adjacent parking
Narrow steep staircases

Ground floor

Upper level

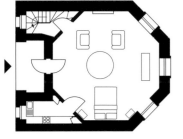

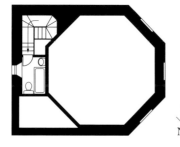

N

# Bath Tower

Caernarfon, Gwynedd

This is one of the towers of the medieval town wall, facing the Menai Strait. More recently, it was part of a Public Bath House, built in 1823 to attract tourists to the town. The present living room was perhaps a Reading Room. Its two great windows look along the outside of the town wall in one direction, and across the Strait in the other. Here you can have your cake and eat it – the sea at your feet in front and the pleasures of an interesting town at your back.

The tower had been empty for a long time when we bought it. Both entrances are eccentric – one along a narrow alley from the street behind, the other from the sea wall. The character, and inevitably the temperature, of the spacious rooms is stamped by the thick curve of the walls. Below the sitting room, reached by a steep spiral stair, there is a very large room in which you can sleep like soldiers of the Edwardian garrison. But if there are only two of you, you can sleep in seclusion at the top of the tower, with just the sky and the battlements.

From the logbook
*A medieval atmosphere has been achieved without all the discomforts of the period.*

For up to 5 people
Solid fuel stove
Roof platform
No private parking

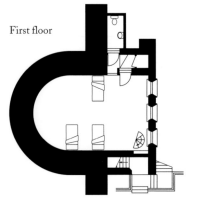

First floor

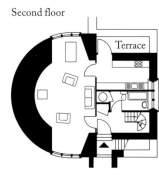

Second floor

Terrace

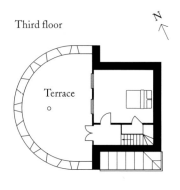

Third floor

Terrace

N

# Beamsley Hospital

Near Skipton, North Yorkshire

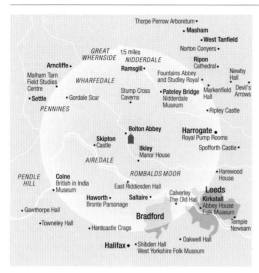

For up to 5 people
Solid fuel stove
Garden

Parking a short
walk away
Dogs allowed

Almshouses are a familiar ingredient in our towns and villages, but the Hospital at Beamsley is more unusual. Set back from the conventional row of dwellings on the main road lies this circular stone building. In it were rooms for seven women, encircling a chapel, through which most of them had to pass to reach their doors, a daily encouragement to piety. Until the 1970s the little community of Mother and Sisters lived here, their lives governed by ancient, and ferociously strict, rules.

The Hospital was founded in 1593 by the Countess of Cumberland, at a time when the poor had only private charity to depend on. Her building is an Elizabethan conceit, alluding both to the six circles, or annulets, on her husband's coat of arms and to the round churches of the Templars. Her daughter, that formidable northern heroine

Lady Anne Clifford, added the front range. She also furnished the chapel and, almshouses being of their nature conservative places, these fittings survive.

Finding the buildings no longer in demand, the Trustees offered them to us. The front range we have let to long-term tenants; and you can stay in the other. Using its oddly shaped rooms and repeatedly crossing the chapel is a curious experience, bringing you close to the subtle yet vigorous Elizabethan mind. And all around is Yorkshire at its highest and most unadulterated.

From the logbook
*So near to so many places to see we could have stayed here for a month – so we will probably come back again and again.*

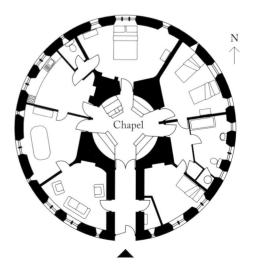

Chapel

N

# Beckford's Tower

Lansdown Road, Bath

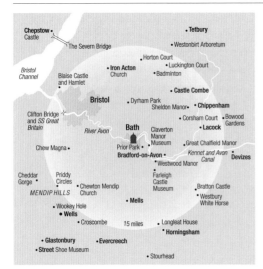

For up to 4 people
Small garden
Adjacent parking

William Beckford (1760–1844) is best known for his extraordinary Gothic folly, Fonthill Abbey in Wiltshire. Its massive central tower, 276 feet high, eventually collapsed taking most of the house with it. Forced by debt to sell Fonthill, he bought two adjacent houses in Lansdown Crescent in Bath, and was soon again pursuing his fascination with towers, building another atop the hill above. This time he chose a more sober style, Greek Revival with a hint of Tuscany.

Born immensely rich, Beckford became a collector, patron, writer and eccentric builder. But he was also indiscreet in his private life, and, cold-shouldered by English Society, he lived in Bath as a recluse. Each morning, accompanied by his dwarf and pack of spaniels, Beckford would ride up to his tower to play with his treasures in its opulent rooms, a reminder of which can be gleaned from the Willes Maddox 'Views' of the Tower c1844, on display in the first floor museum.

After Beckford's death the Tower became a chapel and its grounds an elegant cemetery. More recently two flats, the Tower has now been repaired by the Beckford Tower Trust, who offered us the ground floor. With the proceeds of our Millennium Fund, we have made a Landmark to recreate the layout and something of the flavour of Beckford's interiors, especially in the sumptuous Scarlet Drawing Room. And like him, those who stay here can climb the fine circular staircase to the 'Belvidere' just below the elaborate, gilded lantern and enjoy, all to themselves, what Beckford called "the finest prospect in Europe".

*The museum and the Tower (not the Landmark) will be open to the public on weekends and Bank Holiday Mondays from 10.30–5.00pm between Easter and October, and occasionally by appointment at other times.*

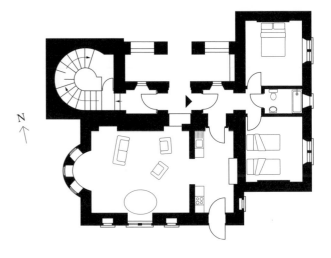

# Brinkburn Mill

Near Rothbury, Northumberland

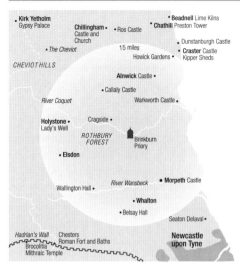

For up to 4 people
Open fire
Garden

Adjacent parking
Dogs allowed

When a priory was founded here in about 1135, the monks, with typical skill, identified one place in this otherwise steep and thickly wooded ravine where there was enough level ground for their buildings. These stood in a loop of the River Coquet, which provided, among other things, water to drive a mill.

The present mill lies at the end of a long lawn, looking back towards the pretty Gothick manor house that stands beside the soaring priory church. This mill was built in about 1800 near the site of its medieval predecessor, but was later dressed up to improve the view from the house. The wheel and grinding stones are still here, although long unused.

At the upper end of the mill, and previously separate from it, are two grander rooms. These may have been an office or perhaps a fishing lodge. One is now the sitting room, with tall windows facing east to catch the morning sun.

Of Brinkburn's setting one historian wrote: 'This is the most deep solitude, chosen for a religious edifice, I ever yet visited'. The same can be said of the mill, reached by its own drive through the woods (once the main approach to the priory) with only the sound of the river for company. An early morning walk among the priory buildings, which are open to the public for part of the year, is recommended.

From the logbook
*That old Landmark magic plus the beauty of Northumberland. As ever, Landmark comes up to and exceeds expectations. Quiet, beautiful, comfortable.*

*The world stopped and we got off and found a place called Brinkburn Mill.*

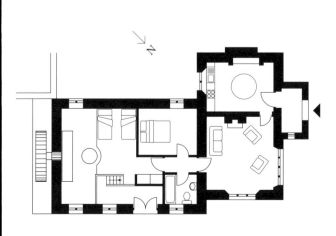

# Bromfield Priory Gatehouse

Near Ludlow, Shropshire

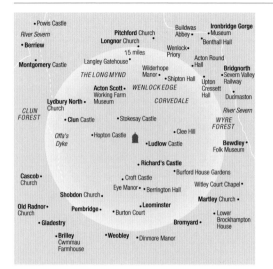

For up to 6 people
Solid fuel stove
Enclosed garden

Parking nearby
Dogs allowed
Steep staircase

The Benedictine monks of Bromfield Priory added a new stone gatehouse to their precinct before 1400. After the Dissolution a timber-framed upper storey was added to this. The room over the arch was used for the manorial court, and later, from 1836 until 1895, for the village school. A teacher's cottage was added at one end and the Gatehouse was largely done up in a Picturesque manner.

Afterwards it became, for many years, the parish reading and recreation room, complete with billiard table, and came in useful for meetings of various sorts, from the youth club to the teaching of first aid. This functional character has rubbed off on the school room itself, which is large and plain and a little formal. At one end, a chimney piece and large cupboards have been put together from an odd assortment of Jacobean carving.

Bromfield itself is an estate village and South Shropshire, with Ludlow as its capital, is deep country still. The Gatehouse now opens on to a grassy churchyard, and the estate office and yard. In front runs a private road, leading only to a few farms and to Oakly Park (the lodge was designed by C. R. Cockerell), successor to the Tudor priory house whose ruins can still be seen on the south side of the parish church.

From the logbook
*A week that seemed to last for eons, full of castles, treasures and untouched countryside.*

*Never before had we encountered Shropshire, or the Landmark Trust, and now we are sure we will become regular visitors to both.*

Ground floor

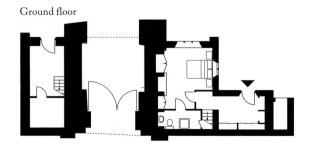

First floor

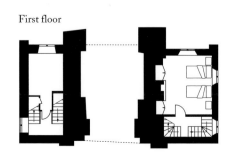

Second floor

# Calverley Old Hall

Calverley, West Yorkshire

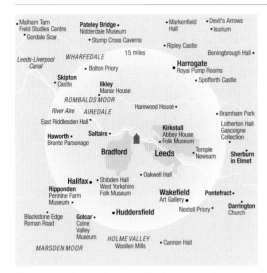

For up to 5 people
Open fire
Enclosed garden

Parking nearby
Dogs allowed

When we arrived on the scene, this ancient house, seat of the Calverley family for over 500 years, had long been divided into cottages and was about to be sold in slices. To save it from this fate, we bought the whole of it and the open ground in front.

The Calverleys were minor Yorkshire magnates, often knighted and latterly baronets. One, put to death after murdering his two eldest sons here (not in the part of the house you stay in) was the subject of a play, The Yorkshire Tragedy, once claimed to be by Shakespeare. Another, it is said, was the model for Sir Roger de Coverley. After the Civil War, the Calverley of the day married the heiress of Esholt Hall, nearby, and from then on the family spent most of their time there.

So Calverley Old Hall went slowly down in the world, and in 1754 was sold to the Thornhills, whose descendants sold it to us. Blackened and stoney in the romantic northern manner, but still quite grand, it is now surrounded by lesser houses. We have so far repaired the chapel, the hammer-beam hall roof and one wing, the North House, in which you can stay.

The close-knit friendly life of the neighbouring streets, of corner shop and pub, soon warms all those who come to Calverley. There are many good things in the area to visit by day, before returning in the evening to ponder, under the moulded beams, on the vanished Calverleys and their once great house.

Ground floor

First floor

# Castle of Park

Glenluce, Dumfries and Galloway

For up to 7 people
Solid fuel stove
Garden

Adjacent parking
Dogs allowed

Thomas Hay was given the lands of Park by his father, the last abbot of Glenluce, and built himself this fine new tower house in 1590. In the 1970s, after standing empty for over a century, the tower was repaired by Historic Scotland, present guardians of Glenluce Abbey. In 1990 they leased the tower to us, and we have made it habitable.

Standing, with two other houses, on a tree-fringed plateau above Luce Bay, the building is outwardly plain. Inside, it is another matter. With the walls plastered and the rooms furnished, you gain a very different impression of the life of a Jacobean laird from that given by the stony shells of so many abandoned towers.

The hall is 30 feet long, with a fine fireplace. From it the laird's private stair leads to bedrooms, each with its own privy (the potential for hide and seek is endless). The wide main stair, in its own tower, has a little room at the top called the cap house, from which you can glimpse the sea.

The eighteenth century brought larger windows to let in more light, the bright clear light of a western peninsula. There are notable gardens to visit nearby, and the rolling fields are grazed by cattle, seemingly more numerous than the human inhabitants.

From the logbook
*We found the Castle of Park warm and comfortable, and the twigs that the jackdaw drops down the sitting-room chimney make great kindling for the stove.*

There is a single bedroom in the cap house, at the top of the stair turret.

Ground floor

Old Kitchen

First floor

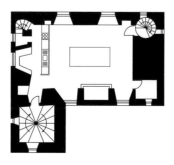

Second floor

Third floor

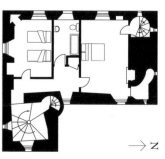

→ N

# Causeway House

For up to 4 people
Gas coal fire

Adjacent parking
Dogs allowed

This is the only house in Northumberland still thatched in heather. Known locally as black thack, it was of course available in abundant supply, but was seldom used once slate became a cheap alternative in the last century. It survived here because the farmhouse, built in 1770 and never much altered, was abandoned over 20 years ago. Used as a store, its thatch was preserved beneath corrugated iron. Lorry loads of heather went into its repair, leaving a cover which is thinner and tougher than conventional thatch. Stuffed into holes in the roof we found two dresses, of about 1890, interesting examples of much worked-in clothing.

Inside, the original arrangement of living room on one side of the cross-wall and byre on the other, with loft over, also survives. The loft is now a warm-weather bedroom, where you can sleep under the knotted tent-like thatch in a fully roofed bed.

The farm, which we own, stands in the rolling fertile land behind Hadrian's Wall. Past the front runs a Roman road, with the stump of a Roman milestone nearby, which gives visitor access within a few hundred yards to the fort and settlement of Vindolanda. Indeed few houses in Britain can have so many traces of Rome around them.

From the logbook
*Settled in immediately; incredibly cosy and welcoming.*

*The heather thatch makes the twin bedroom harder to heat and we do not recommend this room for winter use.*

Ground floor

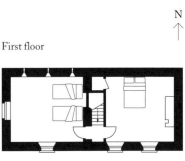

First floor

N

# Cawood Castle

Cawood, near Selby, North Yorkshire

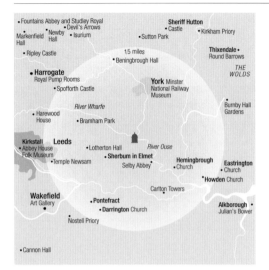

For up to 4 people
Solid fuel stove
Enclosed garden
Roof platform

Adjacent parking
Extremely steep
spiral staircase

This gatehouse, with the domestic wing to one side of it, is all that remains of Cawood Castle, once a stronghold of the Archbishops of York. It stands in the flat land south of York in the small town of Cawood, where there is a bridge over the Ouse. By the fifteenth century, when Archbishop Kempe built our richly decorated gatehouse with two well-proportioned rooms one over the other, it had become less of a castle and more of a palace; his Cardinal's hat, of which he was proud, appears on several of the finely carved stone shields over the archway.

Another cardinal to stay here, just once, was Thomas Wolsey: it was here that he was arrested and turned back to the South where he died soon after. Other visitors include Henry III, Edward I and Queen Margaret, Queen Isabella, and Henry VIII and Queen Catherine (Howard) – not all together, of course.

After the Civil War, Cawood was partially dismantled. In the eighteenth century the

Gatehouse was used as a courtroom and a respectable Georgian staircase was built to supplement the medieval spiral stair.

It was difficult to save these most historic remains because they were divided between two owners; the domestic wing, long used as a barn, was hidden by derelict farm buildings; and part of the gatehouse was in the adjoining dwelling. The first floor room, with handsome bay windows at each end, in fact contained a full-size billiard table (how ever did it get there?) manfully supporting, during all our long negotiations, a huge pile of debris from the collapsed floor above.

In the end our neighbour allowed us to truncate his house a little, and we bought and demolished the farm buildings – so that our visitors can now experience and occupy a late medieval room of the first quality; and in it, if they like, read some history on the spot where it was made.

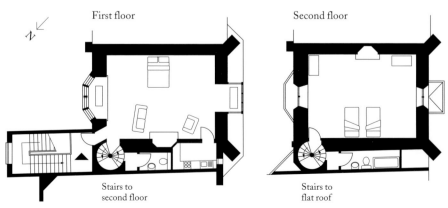

First floor

Second floor

Stairs to
second floor

Stairs to
flat roof

# The Château

Gate Burton, Lincolnshire

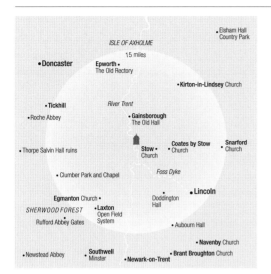

For up to 3 people    Garden
Open fire                 Adjacent parking

This is the earliest recorded building by John Platt of Rotherham, designed in 1747 when he was 19 and almost his only work outside Yorkshire, where he practised and prospered for the next 50 years.

It stands on a grassy knoll above a big bend of the River Trent, on the edge of Gate Burton park. Built as a Gainsborough lawyer's weekend retreat, and later used for picnics and other mild kinds of excursion, it had since been altered and then neglected. Its present owner gave us a long lease of it.

We have restored the Château to its original elaborate and slightly French appearance, an ornament in the landscape, which shows up well from the road some distance away. John Platt must have been a talented young man, because it is difficult to realise until one is inside just how small the scale of the building is; apart from the principal room upstairs, which has a high coved ceiling, there is little space in which to swing a cat. But there are fine views across the park and up a shining reach of the River Trent, along which big slow barges, piling the water in front of them, press on towards an enormous power station, whose cooling towers steam majestically in the distance.

From the logbook
*I feel like Beatrix Potter's mice, living in a very up-market dolls' house.*

First floor

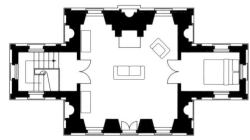

Ground floor

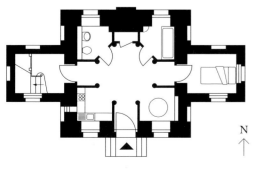

N
↑

# Church Cottage

Llandygwydd, Cardiganshire

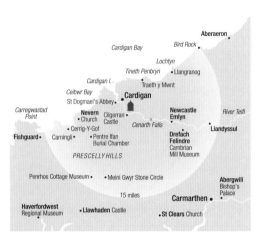

For up to 4 people
Open fire
Garden

Adjacent parking
Dogs allowed

Church Cottage is early Victorian, modestly Gothic, and made of Cilgerran slate. It was also the first Landmark acquired in 1965. The church itself, which was rebuilt in 1857 by R. J. Withers, a prolific architect and committed Ecclesiologist, was demolished in 2000, but its footprint and font remain, as does the churchyard. Our cottage was for the caretaker; it stands in a small village east of Cardigan, in a hilly, well-wooded countryside of small farms. It is also the first building we ever tackled.

Though less than a mile from the main Newcastle Emlyn to Cardigan road, Llandygwydd is quiet, although there is a small road between the cottage and the church. Plays in Cardigan are recommended; so are the coracle races on the Teifi. The south sweep of Cardigan Bay is less than ten miles away; however, the point of Church Cottage is not to dash about, but simply to be there, in this distant and unremarkable part of Wales, and feel what it is like.

From the logbook
*We found lots and lots to do and never strayed outside a five mile radius from the house. Super walks and we managed to wangle a go in a coracle one evening.*

*We brought our dinghy and sailed on most days in Cardigan Estuary.*

*It was a joy to see hart's tongue ferns growing in the bank outside the bathroom window.*

First floor

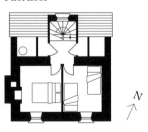

N

Ground floor

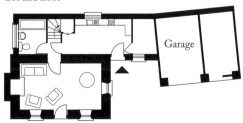

Garage

# Cloth Fair

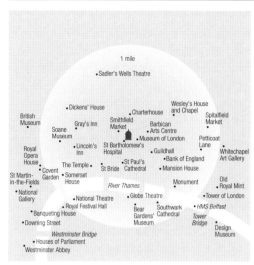

These plain Georgian houses over shops face the churchyard of St Bartholomew the Great, which almost alone among City churches escaped the Great Fire of 1666. They were sold to us by the late Paul Paget, who had rescued them many years before, with No. 41, the only remaining house in the City built before the Fire. Round the corner is Smithfield market with its robust architecture, sights and smells, facing the noble buildings of St Bartholomew's Hospital. Further along Cloth Fair are new houses, bringing domestic life to this part of the City.

There is here a lingering feel of how alive the whole City of London once was before it was destroyed by money, fire and war – a place where long-established institutions, trades, houses, markets and people of all kinds were mingled together. Each of our houses has a respectable staircase, pleasant rooms and nice old joinery. No. 43 was long the home of Sir John Betjeman.

From the logbook
*This house is a remarkable oasis in central London, particularly at the weekend.*

*The whole ambience of the flat in this historic part of the City of London was restful and pleasing to the eye, as well as having all the comfort of 'mod cons'.*

*History comes alive when you stay at Cloth Fair.*

*Cycling from Cloth Fair… puts Soho, Covent Garden and Westminster within ten minutes (and the far end of Hyde Park within twenty) so we had a lovely ride on Christmas morning down to Buckingham Palace.*

No. 43
For up to 2 people
Gas coal fire
Small roof terrace
No private parking

No. 45a
For up to 4 people
Gas coal fire
No private parking

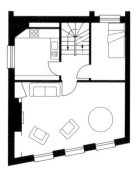

No. 43

No. 43 First floor

Second floor

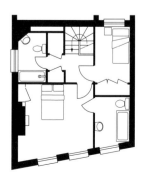

No. 45a First floor

Second floor

# Clytha Castle

Near Abergavenny, Monmouthshire

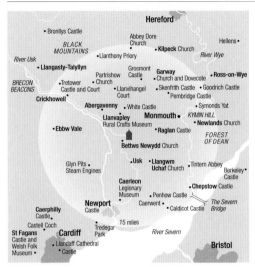

For up to 6 people
Open fire
Garden
Roof platform

Adjacent parking
Steep spiral stairs
Dogs allowed

'Erected in the year 1790 by William Jones of Clytha House, husband of Elizabeth, last surviving child of Sir William Morgan of Tredegar, it was undertaken with the purpose of relieving a mind afflicted by the loss of a most excellent wife, to the memory of whose virtues this tablet is dedicated'.

This most affecting folly, which we lease from the National Trust, stands on the summit of a small hill, at the edge of a grove of old chestnuts. It was designed by a little-known architect and garden designer, John Davenport, perhaps with help from his client. Besides being an eye-catcher, the castle was used for grand picnics and as a retreat; the square tower contains fine rooms on both floors. When we arrived it had been empty for 25 years and before that had housed a gamekeeper. It has the air of a place that has been both loved and neglected. We hope that once again it will relieve the minds of those who come here.

From the logbook
*Seeing my daughter have the time of her life in this fairy-tale castle will live in my memory.*

*A perfect honeymoon destination for us; romantic and secluded.*

*This is our 3rd visit to Clytha and each visit is better than the last.*

*My first Landmark but hopefully not the last although I think Clytha Castle will take some beating.*

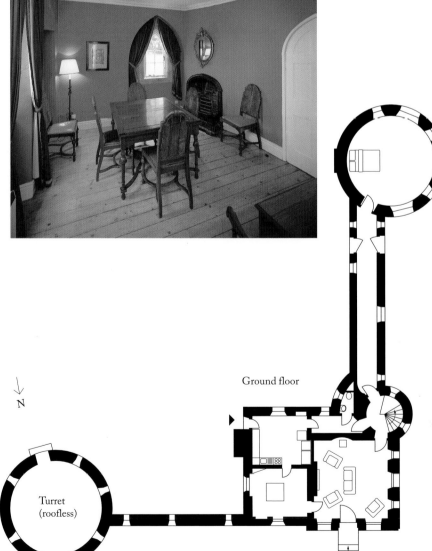

First floor

N

This bedroom is on the second floor

Turret (roofless)

Ground floor

# The College

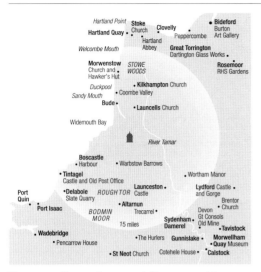

For up to 5 people
Open fire
Enclosed garden

Adjacent parking
Steep staircase
Dogs allowed

When we looked at this house, on the suggestion of one of our visitors, it quickly became clear that it is only part of something that was once much larger, fragments of which appear in the walls and outbuildings around it. These, it turned out, are the remains of a remarkable school, almost the first to be founded by a woman.

Moreover, the woman who founded it, Thomasine Bonaventure, was herself remarkable. Though born here in Cornwall, she married, in turn, three London merchants, each of whom died leaving her his property. This she gave or left to charity, amongst many other benefactions, founding this school in 1506 at the place of her birth.

To oversee the building work, Thomasine appointed her first cousin, John Dinham of Wortham Manor, 12 miles away and today also a Landmark (see Wortham Manor). He remodelled his own house at about the same time, and the two buildings have much in common – notably their carved granite doorways.

Unfortunately, Thomasine also decreed that the master (with an Oxford or a Cambridge degree, and six weeks holiday a year) should pray for the souls of her husbands, a practice firmly disapproved of by the new Protestant regime; and so, as a chantry, it was dissolved two years later. Thus the College at Week St Mary, one of the oldest English schools, prosperously founded, survives only in its name, which still clings to this house more than 300 years later.

The College faces a small courtyard off the village street. Behind it a meadow slopes down to a chequer-work of little fields, and over them appears, black and afar, the high outline of Dartmoor, beyond which Thomasine ventured to such purpose.

From the logbook
*Everyone should get the chance to stay in a Landmark – they're so good for the soul.*

*As always the logbooks have been fascinating. They record the changes to the village over the past two decades.*

Ground floor

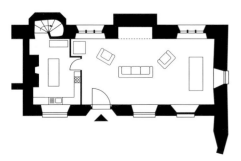

First floor

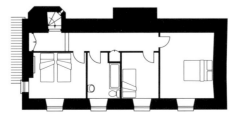

# Coombe

Morwenstow, near Bude, Cornwall

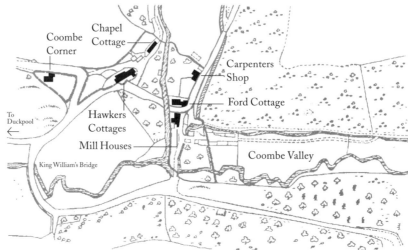

Eight cottages, one for 3, four for 4,
one for 5 and two for 6.

Coombe hamlet consists of a watermill, the
mill house and several cottages, built among
orchards round a ford on a shallow stream.
It is at the junction of two wooded valleys
and is half a mile from the sea at Duckpool,
where a sandy beach is exposed at half tide.

Although a small and humble place,
Coombe has notable connections. On the
hill to the south is Stowe Barton, where the
Grenville family lived for 600 years.
Interesting traces remain of their great house,
demolished in 1739. From soon after 1600
they owned part of Coombe, and its mill was
sometimes called Stowe Mill.

Coombe is partly in the parish of
Morwenstow, and its most famous vicar, the
Reverend Stephen Hawker, lived here for a
short time. He was the inventor (or perhaps
reviver) of harvest festivals, and a moving
spirit in the saving of life at sea. The Reverend
Sabine Baring-Gould ('Onward Christian
Soldiers') wrote a life of Hawker. We have
managed to get enough copies of this book, by
one famous and unusual parson about another,
to put one in most of the cottages at Coombe.

We acquired the whole hamlet as part of
a joint scheme with the National Trust to
preserve it and its exceptional setting. It is a
sheltered place, lying well back from the sea.

Almost all the surrounding land, including
much of the coast (geologically one of the
most impressive in Britain), belongs to the
National Trust. There are long and excellent
walks in all directions. The Mill itself, still
with all its machinery, is a handsome and
interesting stone building with a fine wheel.

From the logbook
*This has to be one of the most unspoilt corners
of Cornwall.*

*A day lasts forever here.*

*A wonderful week – we surfed every day at Duckpool.*

# The Carpenter's Shop

The Carpenter's Shop was where a family of carpenters called Tape carried on their trade from the early nineteenth century. Much of their work must have come from the Stowe estate, which perhaps helped them put up this handsome workshop in about 1830. When we came to Coombe it had been derelict for many years. Our architect, the late Paul Pearn, took pains to preserve its spare and functional character in the new arrangement: a large living-room open to the roof and two bedrooms leading off a gallery, reached by a spiral stair. The living-room has a slate floor and an open fire, formerly the forge. The doors open on to a large old orchard leading down to the stream.

For up to 4 people
Open fire
Shared orchard garden
Adjacent parking
Narrow spiral staircase
Dogs allowed

Ground floor
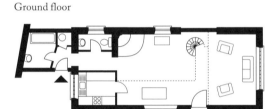

First floor
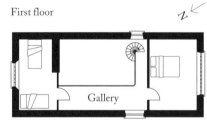

Gallery

# Chapel Cottage

Chapel Cottage takes its name from the former Bible Christian meeting room, which is now its living-room. Made of timber, it arrived in Coombe in about 1860 on wheels, which are still there under the front. These movable 'iron chapels' as they were known could be bought second-hand, which must have suited the pockets of the farm workers who made up the congregation. Once here, it was given a slate roof but fell out of use soon after 1900 and was later divided up and a bungalow added at one end. We restored the chapel itself, putting back its sash windows and timber lining, and improved the appearance and interior of the addition. It is very well placed – a little above the rest of Coombe, looking across the valley over the top of one of the orchards.

For up to 4 people
Solid fuel stove
Small garden
Parking nearby
Dogs allowed

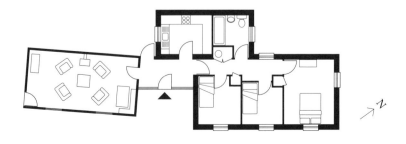

# Coombe

## Coombe Corner

Coombe Corner was built on a hillside above
the rest of the village in the 1930s. With its
painted weatherboarding and large windows
it represents a completely different approach
to building, and to living, to the solid old
houses of Coombe itself. Here life is all about
enjoyment of the weather, of the Cornish
coast, of the view, in a way that could scarcely
be imagined by ordinary hard-working people
even 50 years earlier. Simple bungalow it is,
but made with discretion, forcing itself on no
one. We bought it to round off our ownership
of Coombe and to ensure that it was not
replaced by something less well-mannered, an
all too likely possibility.

For up to 6 people
Solid fuel stove
Garden
Adjacent parking
Dogs allowed

## Ford Cottage

Ford Cottage is an extremely old cottage of
cob and thatch on the edge of the stream,
close to Mill House. Teas used to be served
here. It has a large high living-room with a
slate floor and solid fuel stove. It opens onto
a large orchard at the back, running
alongside the stream.

For up to 4 people
Solid fuel stove
Shared orchard garden
Adjacent parking
Dogs allowed

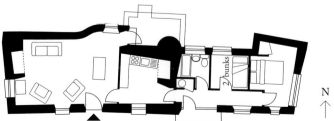

# Hawkers Cottages

Hawkers Cottages are a pair of stone, cob and thatched cottages, named after the famous Vicar of Morwenstow, who lived here briefly. The bedroom in No. 1, with a window in the form of a cross, is said to have been his study. No. 2 is slightly larger and has a handsome living-room with a slate floor and a particularly splendid old cupboard made by the carpenter at Coombe. The small gardens in front of both cottages are sheltered and pretty.

No. 1
for up to 5 people
No. 2
for up to 6 people

Solid fuel stoves
Small gardens
Adjacent parking
Dogs allowed

No. 1

No. 2

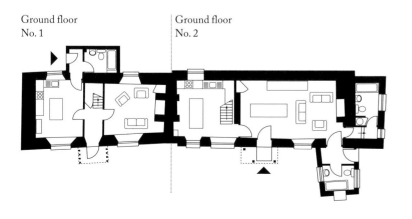

Ground floor
No. 1

Ground floor
No. 2

First floor
No. 1

First floor
No. 2

# Coombe

## Mill House

Mill House dates from before 1700, with later additions, and is divided into two. It is mainly built of stone, with patches of cob, a massive chimney and a thatched and slated roof. The Tape family, living here at the turn of the twentieth century, was a large and musical one, whose children would sing in the evenings or play on the piano, the cornet and the violin. The sitting-room of No. 1, with its wide fireplace, has changed very little since that time. A shallow stream, which you can sit and watch or wade in, runs past a cobbled terrace at the back.

From the logbook
*The clocks changed last weekend but we didn't find out till Wednesday.*

*A kingfisher stopped by for breakfast.*

*We got colour on our faces on a day-trip to Lundy, which is highly recommended.*

No. 1
for up to 4 people
No. 2
for up to 3 people

Open fires
Adjacent parking
Dogs allowed

No. 1

No. 2

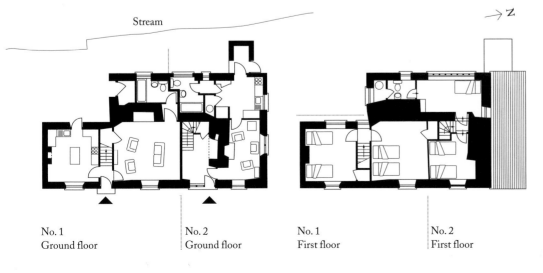

Stream

| No. 1 | No. 2 | No. 1 | No. 2 |
| Ground floor | Ground floor | First floor | First floor |

# Coop House

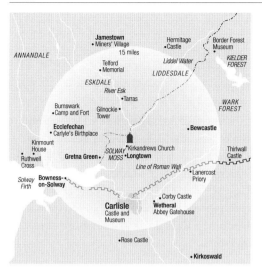

For up to 3 people
Solid fuel stove
Garden

Narrow spiral
staircase

This building serves to remind us of a progressive landowner's efforts in a remote and beautiful place. It stands on the bank of the River Esk, on a high unfenced platform once at the end of a stone weir, in front of which coops or traps were set to catch salmon. This was just one of many improvements made to his estate by Dr Robert Graham of Netherby in the 1760s and '70s. Another was to build this summerhouse as an ornament in the landscape around Netherby Hall and as a place to enjoy the river.

Coop House was to prove the more lasting. The river broke up the weir and only blocks of masonry are left, strewn on the river bed. It had in any case annoyed the Scots upstream who, deprived of their salmon catch, marched on Netherby in force – a scene described by Sir Walter Scott in Redgauntlet.

Having been for some time an estate cottage, Coop House was given up in 1936 as too remote. By the 1980s it had partly fallen down. The Grahams, who still own Netherby, gave us a lease, and we have laid a long and many-gated track and rebuilt its polygonal main room. With its three windows, this room is designed for watching the Esk as it flows past, sometimes gentle, sometimes in spate. Your nearest neighbours, a little way upstream on the opposite bank, are a pele tower and a graceful Georgian church. Behind are watermeadows, with the imposing pile of Netherby Hall in the distance.

From the logbook
*The river is a wonderful companion.*

Ground floor

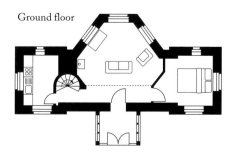

First floor

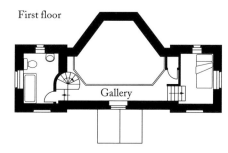

Gallery

# Crownhill Fort

Plymouth, Devon

For up to 8 people
Enclosed grounds

Open fire
Adjacent parking

In the 1860s it was decided to protect naval bases such as Plymouth from attack by land as well as by sea. A chain of forts was built, with Crownhill in the key position in the north of the city. It is now one of only two large works of this kind in the country to remain in good condition.

From a distance, the Fort blends with the hilltop, defended not by walls but by steep earth ramparts. These enfold the central parade ground, around which are handsome quarters for up to 300 men. For further protection, the buildings and many of the emplacements for 32 large guns have turf roofs, some restored by us. Outside the ramparts is a deep dry ditch, 30 feet wide at the bottom, which could be covered by protective fire from a chemin de ronde and six three-storey caponiers, reached from inside the fort by long tunnels.

Since acquiring the Fort in 1987, we have done major work to grounds, weaponry, and buildings, many of which are now let to small businesses. In 1995 the Fort was opened to the public for the first time; and in 1998 it was once again armed with a Moncrieff Disappearing Gun, the only working example in the world.

Crownhill fascinates the enthusiast and the novice alike. It is also a remarkably pleasant place to be. The Officers' Quarters in which you stay face south, the kitchen with a large window and a commanding view of the comings and goings. Above all, you have the free run of this spectacular structure of stone and earth.

From the logbook
*It's so peaceful in the evenings; no sound of traffic – you could be miles from a city.*

*There is something about going in and out through the mighty entrance that makes you feel noble and British.*

The Fort is open to the public from 1 April to 31 October, Sunday to Friday, 10am to 5pm. It is open all year round for groups by appointment, corporate and private hire, including civil wedding ceremonies.

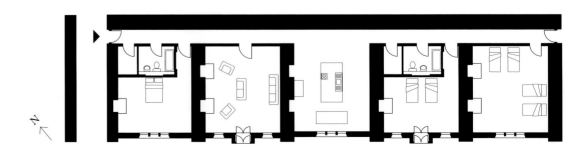

# Culloden Tower

For up to 4 people
Open fire
Small fenced garden
Roof platform

Parking nearby
Steep spiral staircase
Dogs allowed

This tower was built in 1746 by John Yorke, MP for Richmond, and named to mark the final establishment of Hanoverian rule after the defeat of the Jacobites in the same year. It stands in the park of his long-demolished house, at the edge of a steep slope above the River Swale, on the site of an old pele tower. It was probably designed by Daniel Garrett, also architect of The Banqueting House.

Inside are to be found, one above the other, two tall octagonal rooms, flooded with daylight and of the highest quality. The carving and plaster work of the lower is in a Gothic style, while that of the upper is Classical. Here you will sleep under what must be our grandest bedroom ceiling, worth all the 60 steps you must climb to reach it.

Neglect and vandals had done a great deal of damage by the time we bought the tower, but old photographs and salvaged fragments made restoration possible. It is difficult to imagine, certainly to find, a more romantic situation, looking over the trees of this park with the sight and sound of the Swale hurrying over its rocks and stones below; and with the particularly handsome town of Richmond, which has an eighteenth century theatre and much more besides, a few hundred yards away.

From the logbook
*This is the most wonderful place I ever stayed in my life!*

*To have a whole Tower to ourselves – along with an unexpected and amazing roof – was perfect!*

*The Tower is wonderful – like staying in a large Wedgwood vase…*

Ground floor

Mezzanine floor

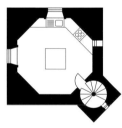

First floor

Second floor

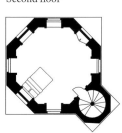

N

# Danescombe Mine

Calstock, Cornwall

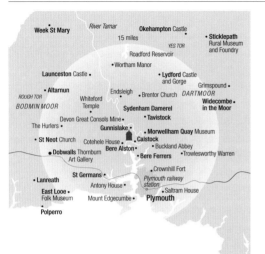

These are the monumental buildings of the old Cotehele Consols' copper and arsenic mine. They are unusually well built, handsome and complete, and stand by a stream in a steep wooded valley leading down to the Tamar. We have taken a long lease of them from the National Trust and have consolidated and repaired them, so that it is possible to stay here in comfort and study at close quarters the tremendous past of the Devon and Cornish mines. It was a dreadful but romantic trade which enriched among others the Dukes of Bedford and the family of William Morris.

The engine house, which we have made habitable, is strongly built of the Killas stone in which the lodes occur. It used to contain a rotary beam engine with a 40-inch cylinder driving a Taylor roll crusher, a pump and two buddles on the dressing floor. The mine worked, on and off, from 1822 to 1900, kept alive at the last by the demand for arsenic to protect cotton against the boll weevil.

In the woods above lie the abandoned shafts of other mines; and only a short and beautiful walk away, above the Tamar, is Cotehele, a most notable medieval house.

From the logbook
*My favourite Landmark!! Excellent building, wonderful surroundings, beautifully kept – all the superlatives. Sleeping in the top bedroom is like being in a tree house.*

For up to 4 people
Wooden decking
Parking nearby

Steep open staircases
Dogs allowed

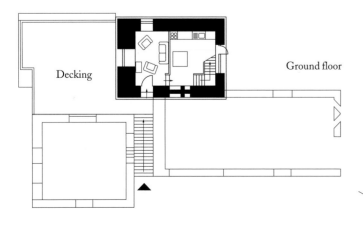

Decking

Ground floor

First floor

Second floor

# Dolbelydr

Great Orme Country Park
Liverpool
Llandudno
Colwyn Bay
Rhyl
Gwrych Castle
St Asaph Cathedral
Bodnant Gardens
Vale of Clwyd
Flint Castle
Vale of Conwy
CLWYDIAN RANGE
Ewloe Castle
River Dee
Denbigh Castle
Llanrwst Bridge
Moel Fammau
George III Jubilee Tower
Mold Church
Hawarden Castle Park
Gwydir Chapel and Castle
Swallow Falls
DENBIGH MOORS
Llyn Bran
Ruthin Castle
Betws-y-coed Bridge
SNOWDONIA
Alwen Reservoir
Derwen
Churchyard Cross
Wrexham Church
Erddig
River Conwy
15 miles
Rug Chapel
Caer Drewyn Hillfort
Valle Crucis Abbey
Corwen
Llangollen
Plas Newydd
Pont Cysyllte Aqueduct
River Dee
Chirk Castle

For up to 6 people       Adjacent parking
Open fire                      Steep stairs
Enclosed garden          Dogs allowed

Henry VIII had much to answer for, and for some who live west of the Welsh Marches, not the least of his errors was the imposition of English as the language of government throughout his kingdom. Yet Welsh scholars rose to the challenge of the Tudor regimes, among them humanist and physician Henry Salesbury. Dolbelydr was the family manor and in 1593, Salesbury published his *Grammatica Britannica*, written in this fine stone house in the pastoral valley of the River Elwy. By imposing a classical discipline on the grammar of this ancient language, his work gives Dolbelydr some claim to be the birthplace of modern Welsh.

The house was built in 1579; when we found it, it had endured a gradual slide from its gentry status, into decades of neglect which had left it finally floorless and roofless. Yet some rare primary features remained, including fine timber mullioned windows. We found the newel post from the original spiral staircase reused in a later one and careful analysis of the building allowed us to reinstate not only this spiral staircase but also the plank-and-muntin screen in their original positions.

On the basis of such survivals, we have taken the house back to its original form, to present a high status sixteenth century gentry home much as Henry Salesbury would have known it, with first floor solar open to the roof beams and high courtyard walls typical of Denbighshire. Here you may cook and eat communally in the hall, before retiring for civilised conversation to the chamber above, just as the Salesburys would have done. One translation of Dolbelydr is 'Meadow of the Rays of the Sun', an accurate description when the sunlight slants across the valley floor. It is not difficult for the centuries to fall away as you gaze through mullioned windows down this tranquil valley, shared only with the sheep and the deer and the sound of the Elwy.

From the logbook
*Dolbelydr is a sanctuary standing solitary in its timeless valley.*

Ground floor

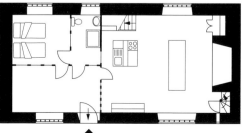

First floor

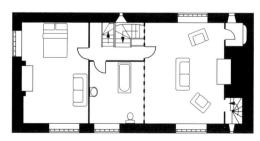

Second floor

N

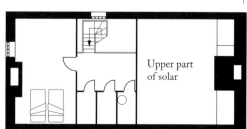

Upper part of solar

# Edale Mill

Edale, Derbyshire

For up to 4 people
Parking nearby

This cotton mill was built in the late eighteenth century, and during the whole of its long working life survived the hazards of finance and fire, to both of which such mills were prone. After 1800 it was extended at each end, and the stone staircase tower was added. When the Manchester to Sheffield railway was built through the Hope valley in the 1890s it became practicable to use coal; the water wheel was removed and the mill was powered by steam until its then owners, Fine Spinners and Doublers Ltd, closed it in 1934.

We bought it in 1969, restored the slate roof and every single window, and divided the interior into seven dwellings, six of which we sold and one of which, on a middle floor, we kept as a Landmark. Our architect took particular trouble with such details as the downpipes, which were specially made for us square in section, making all the difference to the mill's appearance; we took measures to soundproof between floors, though inevitably some noise remains; and we put cables underground. In spite of these apparent extravagances the whole project turned out to be economic and the mill, instead of being demolished, now remains, we hope, an ornament to the dale and a monument to those who laboured in it.

From the logbook
*We went for a long walk, twelve miles or so, through Edale village, up the stream to the moor and along it to the Roman track.*

*Generally, my husband stayed in and read about the walks while I went out and did them.*

*The right combination of luxury and puritanism.*

*Just imagine it with all the looms clattering away.*

The Landmark apartment is at the right-hand end of the mill building, on the second floor.

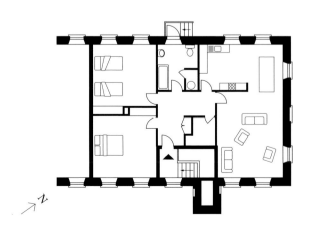

# The Egyptian House

Chapel Street, Penzance, Cornwall

One apartment for 3
and two for 4
*First floor*
for up to 3 people
*Second floor*
for up to 4 people
*Third floor*
for up to 4 people

Gas coal fires
No private parking
Narrow oval staircase

This is a rare and noble survivor of a style that enjoyed a vogue after Napoleon's campaign in Egypt of 1798. It dates from about 1835 and the front elevation is very similar to that of the former Egyptian Hall in Piccadilly, designed in 1812 by P. F. Robinson. Robinson or Foulston of Plymouth are the most likely candidates for its design, though there is no evidence to support the claim of either.

It was built for John Lavin as a museum and geological repository. When we bought it in 1968, its colossal façade, with lotus bud capitals and enrichments of Coade stone, concealed two small granite houses above shops, solid and with a pleasant rear elevation, but very decrepit inside. In the course of our work to the front, we reconstructed these as three compact apartments, the highest of which has a view through a small window of Mounts Bay and St Michael's Mount, over the chimney pots of the town.

Why was there a geological shop here? Although picked over by the Victorians (doubtless including Mr Lavin) the beaches at Penzance still hold every kind of pebble, from quartz to chalcedony. Penzance itself, accessible by train as well as by road, is a handsome and agreeable town; and beyond it lies that hard old peninsula in which, at places like Chysauster and the Botallack mine, can be found moving evidence of human labour, over an immense span of time.

From the logbook
*No photograph or drawing can depict the astonishing and eccentric elevation of the Egyptian House.*

*Arriving and departing by train we made extensive use of the coastal bus system to travel wherever we wanted to go.*

*We've enjoyed our 'Flight into Egypt'.*

*Visit no 7 over a 15 year period – our first Landmark and still our favourite.*

*We much appreciated the furniture and delighted in the witty Egyptian motifs.*

First floor

First floor

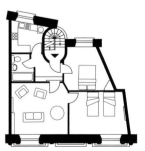

Second floor

Third floor

→ N

# Elton House

Abbey Street, Bath

For up to 10 people
Small walled garden

No private parking

Elton House overlooks Abbey Green, in the centre of Bath. It was given to us, with much desirable furniture, by Miss Philippa Savery, a gallant campaigner for the city's preservation. The earliest part of it dates from just before 1700, but it was subsequently enlarged and re-fronted, becoming by 1750 a handsome robust building on several floors, with a fine staircase and excellent joinery, arranged as sets of lodgings. Thereafter the fashionable world moved up the hill, away from Abbey Green; part of the ground floor became a shop and the rest of the house stayed as it was. It is therefore something of a rarity, even for Bath.

From the logbook
*Beautiful house close to everything you need to see in the centre of Bath. Felt as though I belonged to the city for a weekend.*

*Bath kept us well entertained for the whole week.*

*Elton House is a large historic house which manages to feel intimate and welcoming.*

*Walks to Beckford's Tower… the American museum at Claverton… the Sham Castle.*

First floor
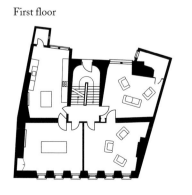

Second floor

Third floor

# Endsleigh

Near Tavistock, Devon

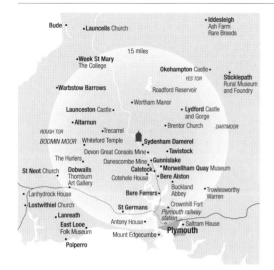

This most naturally beautiful stretch of the River Tamar (Turner, among others, sketched here and called it 'altogether Italian') was chosen by Georgiana, Duchess of Bedford, as the setting for a new house; between 1810 and 1816 both Humphrey Repton and Jeffrey Wyatville played a part in shaping it to perfection, and in placing suitable buildings within it.

Endsleigh today is still a very complete example of that most imaginative and English taste, the Picturesque. From the 1950s, most of it was leased and then owned by a fishing syndicate, who used the main house, known as the Cottage, as a fishing lodge-cum-hotel and did much to restore the garden and arboretum. Other parts of the woods were sold separately, and it was inevitable that unfunctional buildings should suffer. It was to save some of them that we became involved. Then, in 2004, the fishing syndicate decided that it was no longer feasible for it to maintain so large an estate and so the Cottage and grounds were sold for use as a discreet private hotel. Our two Landmarks, safe within their freehold tenure, are sufficiently secluded to be unaffected by such changes in ownership and continue their tranquill existence.

## Pond Cottage

In 1983 we took on the Dairy, a strongly Picturesque building, and with it Pond Cottage, previously used by visiting fishermen (you too can fly-fish in the pond). Both buildings were designed by Wyatville, but the idea for creating 'Dairy Dell', with its streams and cascades, its still dark pond and overhung ancient well, was Repton's, proposed in his *Red Book* for Endsleigh.

Pond Cottage has a Rustic porch, with tree-trunk columns and honeysuckle, and cosy rooms. The Dairy, which had to be rescued from the undergrowth, is perched on a knoll above, a cool chamber of marble (a local variety) and ivy-leaf tiles. From its verandah, 'embosomed', as Repton put it, 'in all the sublimity of umbrageous majesty', you may open yourself to those keen responses to the surrounding scene that were so carefully planned by its creators – while contemplating the making of a very superior butter.

For up to 5 people
Open fire
Parking a short walk away
Garden with stream and pond
Dogs allowed

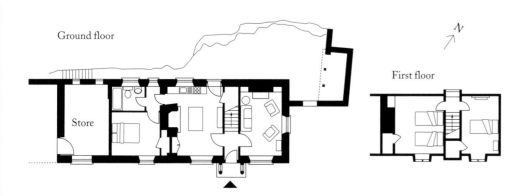

Ground floor

Store

First floor

# Endsleigh

## Swiss Cottage

In 1977 we bought Swiss Cottage, perhaps the most important of Endsleigh's buildings. It is an early, and wonderfully well-made, example of the nineteenth-century passion for the Alps, designed in about 1815 by Wyatville, complete with an Alpine garden, and Swiss furniture and crockery. We repaired it and reversed some later alterations. The main room, opening on to a verandah, was used by the Dukes for picnics and shooting lunches and there, perched high above the steep drop to the river, you have a heady feeling of surveying a world apart.

For up to 4 people
Steep garden
Low ceiling on top floor
Parking a short walk away
Dogs allowed

Ground floor

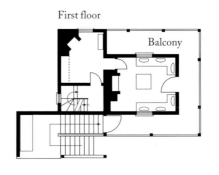

First floor

Balcony

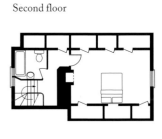

Second floor

# Field House

For up to 7 people
Open fire
Enclosed garden

Adjacent parking
Dogs allowed

This handsome stone house was left to us with the surrounding land by Miss Eileen Jenkins, who had lived here for the previous 20 years. It is an unusual building, since although it looks like a single house, and indeed has been one for over a century, it was clearly once four separate dwellings round a narrow yard, each with one room up and one down. But by 1884 the yard had been roofed over and filled with a staircase, and the whole building became one farmhouse.

The thick party walls of the old dwellings give Field House a pleasant solid feel inside. It stands in a large and sheltered walled garden (still cared for by Miss Jenkins' gardener) high up on the top of the Cotswolds, once a land of sheep but now more given over to the horse.

From the logbook
*Our seventh Landmark and the most comfortable and child friendly.*

*Enjoyed our stay at Field House thoroughly, especially eating the ripe figs from the tree in the garden for breakfast and blackberries from the hedge.*

*The honeysuckle was marvellous – its perfume filled my bedroom in the mornings.*

*We really found it difficult sometimes to leave Field House and garden to explore more of the Cotswolds.*

Ground floor

First floor

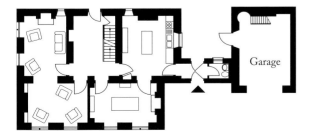

Garage

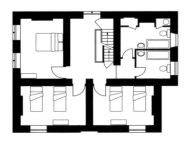

There is a single bedroom up a steep staircase in the attic (not shown).

→ N

# Fort Clonque

Alderney, Channel Islands

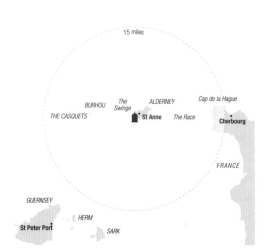

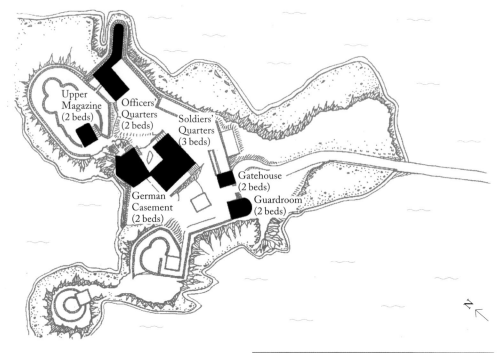

For up to 13 people
Open fires
Dogs allowed
The island can be cut
off at high tide

There are frequent
flights to Alderney
from Southampton

In the 1840s it was thought that the advent of steam would make the Channel Islands more important as an advanced naval base, and also more liable to capture by the French. Accordingly the great harbour works of Alderney were begun in 1847. Fort Clonque, the most remarkable of them, occupies a group of large rocks off the steep south-west tip of the island, commanding the passage between it and Burhou. It is reached by a causeway leading to a drawbridge entrance and was originally designed for ten 64-pounder guns in four open batteries, manned by two officers and 50 men.

Very soon, however, the further develop-ment of steam brought the Channel Islands within easy reach of mainland bases, and made another in Alderney unnecessary. In 1886 the Defence Committee recommended that Clonque, and all the other works except Fort Albert, should be disarmed but left standing.

It was thus that Hitler found them in 1940 and, imagining again that the Channel Islands had strategic value, vigorously refortified them. At Fort Clonque part of the Victorian soldiers' quarters was replaced by an enormous casemate, housing a gun so large that its emplacement now makes a handsome bedroom looking towards Guernsey.

Most forts are of necessity large and grim, but Clonque, because it has had to be fitted to the great rocks round which it is built, is small,

open and picturesque, ingeniously contrived on many levels, with stretches of grass, samphire and mesembryanthemum here and there. Any cold or damp, characteristic of such a fort, will be more than compensated for by the delight of its spectacular setting. (The clean air allows all sorts of lichen to grow on the granite walls.) On calm days the sea can be heard all round, restlessly searching the rocks; and on rough days it is comforting to reflect that the wall of the East Flank Battery is 19 feet thick. During some high tides the fort is cut off and the sea runs between it and the mainland.

The marine views are second to none – of the other islands, rocks and stacks; of two great colonies of gannets, which fish round the fort; of the lighthouses on the Casquets; and of the formidable race or current called the Swinge, which runs between Clonque and Burhou.

On all counts Fort Clonque is a most worthwhile place to have tackled, not least because when we embarked on it in 1966 military works such as this were disregarded everywhere. The rest of Alderney is also extremely pleasant; the island is just small enough to be explored entirely on foot or, very easily, by bicycle; all the Victorian and German defence works are interesting; the beaches at the north end are exceptional; and in the centre is St Anne, a very pretty little town, English with a hint of France.

From the logbook
*Rarely have I felt so relaxed or comfortable and been somewhere so beautiful.*

*The fort is fantastic, especially during a good blow, when the sky rains sea foam!*

*It was like being in a big granite ocean liner!*

*The cycling on Alderney is fabulous.*

Officers' Quarters

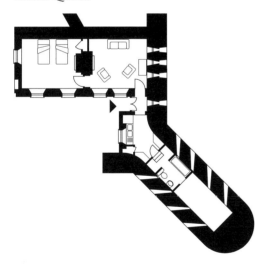

Soldiers' Quarters

There are eight more
beds in other parts
of the fort, as shown
on the plan opposite.

# Fox Hall

Charlton, West Sussex

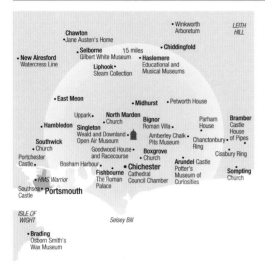

For up to 4 people

Open fire

Garden

Adjacent parking

Charlton is just a small village, but at one time, when the Charlton Hunt was famous and fashionable, its name was familiar and dear to every sportsman in England. Even Goodwood was described as 'near Charlton'. The hunt was founded in the 1670s by the Duke of Monmouth and was continued after his death by his son-in-law the Duke of Bolton and then by the Duke of Richmond.

Apart from the sport, what attracted high-spirited noblemen here, surely, was that they could live in lodgings away from the constraints of home. They clubbed together and built a dining-room for themselves, which they christened 'Fox Hall', designed by Lord Burlington, no less, and here 'these votaries of Diana feasted after the chase and recounted the feats of the day'. Not to miss such affairs and to be in good time for the meets, the Duke of Richmond commissioned the small Palladian building that we now possess. The designer of this rich sample of architecture, built in 1730, was most probably Lord Burlington's assistant Roger Morris.

It consists of a plain brick box with a small stylish hall and staircase leading to one magnificent room above, undoubtedly Britain's premier bed-sit. There is a gilded alcove for the Duke's bed and in the pediment over the fireplace an indicator shows the direction of the wind, important information for the fox hunter. The front door to all this grandeur leads very sensibly straight to the stable yard.

In the 1750s the Hunt was moved away from Charlton to Goodwood. The old Fox Hall disappeared and somehow its name was transferred to our building a few yards off, which, grievously altered, for a long time housed the manager of the Duke of Richmond's sawmill. So far as possible we have given it back its original form.

Apart from Fox Hall, and a detail or two in some of the houses, no visible trace remains at Charlton of the famous Hunt; but the pub is called the Fox Goes Free, a modest clue to great doings here in former times.

Ground floor

First floor

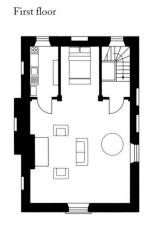

→ N

# Frenchman's Creek

Helford, Cornwall

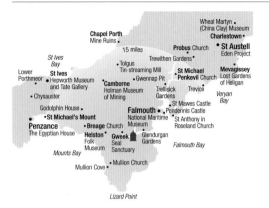

You can see small granite cottages like this in their hundreds in Cornwall, but it would be hard to find one in a more remote, romantic and secluded place than this, tucked down at the head of Frenchman's Creek on the Helford River. It was built in about 1840 for a farm worker or boatman; there were once two more cottages here and a small quay. Between the Wars, it was rented as a retreat by Maria Pendragon and Clara Vyvyan, who describes it in her book *The Helford River*. The last inhabitants moved out a few years ago, and the National Trust, which owns the land around, suggested a joint scheme to us, as the only alternative to letting it fall down.

The Creek, one of many along the shores of the tidal river, runs like a finger, deep into the woods, giving brief sparkling glimpses of water between the trees; at high tide it is passable by boat. The quarter-mile path down to the cottage is steep (and sometimes slippery; you may need to leave your car at the top). In summer you descend into greenness, for the woods are mainly oak, with the light filtered through leaves. It is a place for those who worship the woods and the water and are prepared to be temporarily dominated by them. Should you want to go elsewhere there is the Lizard to explore, and Mounts Bay, or to the east the granite elegance of Falmouth.

For up to 4 people
Open fire
Garden

Parking nearby
Dogs allowed

Ground floor

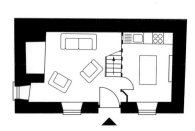

First floor

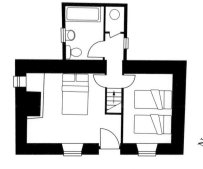

# Freston Tower

Near Ipswich, Suffolk

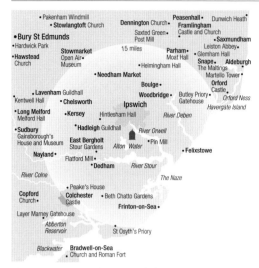

For up to 4 people
Small enclosed
garden

Adjacent parking
Steep spiral staircase
Dogs allowed

Freston Tower was given to Landmark through the great generosity of its owner, who wished it to have a secure future and be enjoyed by many. Set in old and undulating parkland of oaks, sweet chestnuts, cedar and beech trees, the tower was built in the mid 1550s overlooking the broad expanse of the River Orwell estuary. We have yet to discover why or by whom it was built, but its most likely builder was a wealthy Ipswich merchant called Thomas Gooding who bought Freston Manor in 1553.

Freston Tower was built both to admire from the outside and to look out from on the inside – there are no fewer than 26 windows dotted over its six storeys, arranged in careful hierarchy. Its crisp brickwork with distinctive blue diapering suggests that it was always intended to perform as an eyecatcher in the landscape. It may also have acted as a lookout tower for Gooding's returning ships, or simply as an extravagant folly (and if so, one of the earliest in the country). It may even have been built to coincide with Queen Elizabeth's progress to Ipswich in 1561, when the citizens

were warned in advance of 'Perambulacion [of] liberty by water with the Queen. There shall be two vessells or botes decently furnished to attend upon the Queen's Majestie so far as the liberty doe extend.'

Just as it did to build, this carefully designed tower demanded the highest standards of craftsmanship to restore. Using early photographs as sources, we re-rendered the brick mullions and window surrounds in imitation of stone, a building material so lacking in East Anglia.

We chose to put the sitting room on the top floor, to take advantage of unrivalled views of the River Orwell and its handsome modern bridge. Did Sir Thomas Gooding go one stage further, as our visitors may, and sit amid the pinnacles to make a banquet house of the roof? We cannot be sure of this either, but it would certainly be in keeping with the bravura of this fine tower.

From the logbook
*We have enjoyed living vertically for a week – sad to be coming back down to earth.*

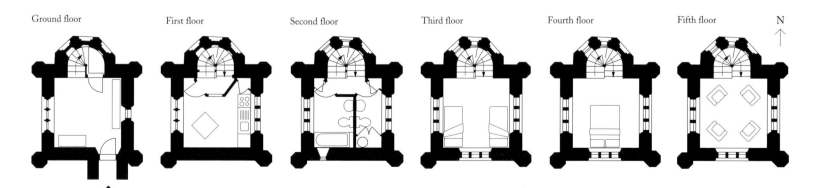

Ground floor    First floor    Second floor    Third floor    Fourth floor    Fifth floor    N

# Gargunnock House

Near Stirling, Central Scotland

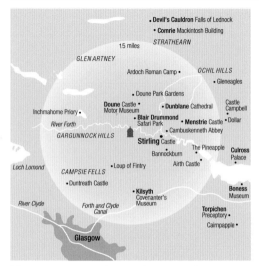

For up to 16 people
Open fires

Large garden
Adjacent parking

The main front of Gargunnock, when approached through the park, looks regular, classical, serenely late Georgian. But this façade of 1794 is only skin deep, imposing order on additions made then and in the previous two centuries to an old tower, which still forms the core of the house.

The old tower also dictates that the main rooms are on the first floor, above the traditional vaulted basement. Of these, unquestionably the finest is the drawing-room; it contains a piano (now ornamental) on which, just possibly, Frédéric Chopin once played. Gargunnock was bought in 1835 by Charles Stirling, a Glasgow merchant and son of an old Perthshire family. His sister, Jane, was Chopin's pupil and friend. She brought him to Scotland in 1848, taking him

to stay with her sisters and cousins, and family tradition is firm that he came here too.

The late Miss Viola Stirling was the last of her family. She left Gargunnock to trustees who now let it, with our help, for holidays. Staying here feels rather as if the family has gone away for a while. They have taken their personal things with them, but the furniture remains, the flower garden is cared for, the park is grazed and the estate maintained in orderly fashion.

There is fine country in all directions, and Stirling is nearby, but most of all you can enjoy living briefly in this graceful and pleasantly old-fashioned country house at the foot of the Gargunnock Hills.

*The gardens are open to the public on Wednesdays in April, May, September and October.*

There is a further
double bedroom,
twin bedroom and
two bathrooms on
the third floor.

First floor

Second floor

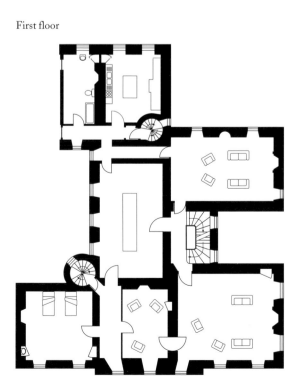

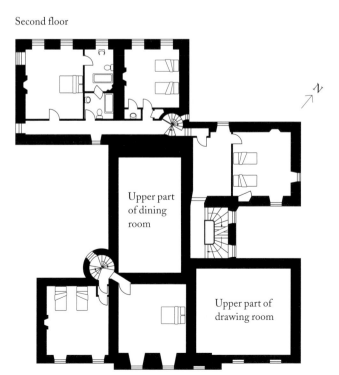

Upper part
of dining
room

Upper part of
drawing room

# Goddards

Abinger Common, Surrey

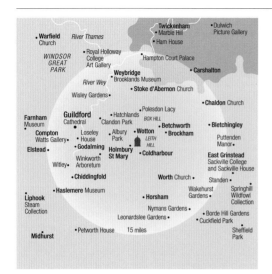

For up to 12 people
Open fire
Large enclosed garden

Adjacent parking
Dogs allowed

Goddards was built by Edwin Lutyens in 1898–1900 and enlarged by him in 1910. It is considered one of his most important early houses, designed in the traditional Surrey style and with a garden, now under restoration, laid out in collaboration with Gertrude Jekyll.

The commission was an unusual one. In the words of Lawrence Weaver, writing on Lutyens' houses in 1913, it was built 'as a Home of Rest to which ladies of small means might repair for holiday'. This was the idea of Frederick Mirrielees, a wealthy businessman who had married an heiress of the Union Castle shipping line. A central range with common rooms on both floors divided two cottages, the southern of which also contained a bowling alley. Here Lutyens played a game of skittles in 1901 with the three nurses and two old governesses then staying here. They all loved the house and 'invariably weep when they leave it'.

In 1910 Mirrielees adapted the house for his son to live in. The upper common room was divided and the cottages were extended to provide large bedrooms over a dining-room and library: two diverging wings, which hold the courtyard garden in loose embrace.

It was in a state little changed from this that the house was given to the Lutyens Trust in 1991 by Mr and Mrs M.W. Hall, its owners since 1953. The Trust, having found its care too costly, has now leased it to us, and it is once again a place to repair to for holidays and skittles. The Lutyens Trust retains the use of the Library.

Goddards stands on a little green, approached by lanes so deeply sunk as to be almost tunnels. Large estates (one of them John Evelyn's Wootton) and the National Trust guard the surrounding country, in whose wooded landscape and brick and tile villages are concealed many masterpieces of the Arts and Crafts movement.

*Part of the ground floor and the garden are open to the public by appointment only on Wednesday afternoons, from the Wednesday after Easter to the last Wednesday in October.*

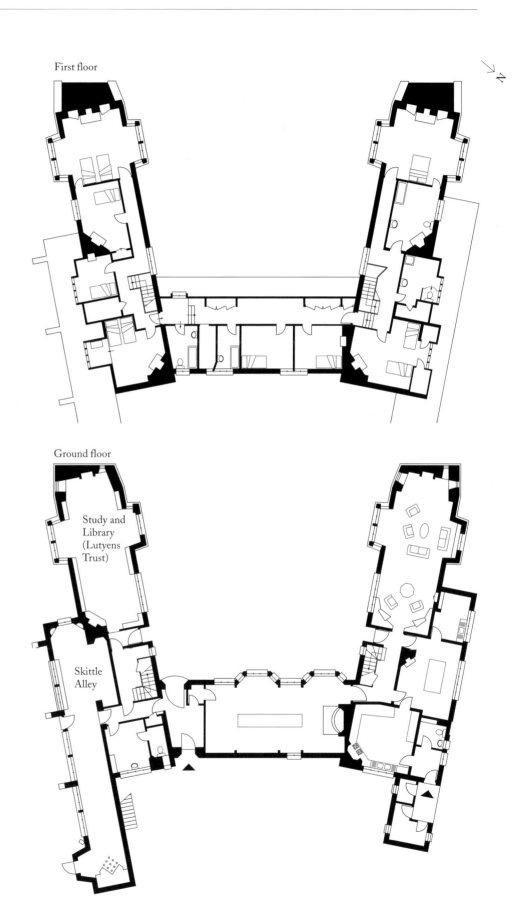

First floor

Ground floor

Study and
Library
(Lutyens
Trust)

Skittle
Alley

# Gothic Temple

Stowe, Buckinghamshire

This temple, built in 1741, is one of the last additions to the garden at Stowe formed for Lord Cobham by Charles Bridgeman and his successor, William Kent. That same year, 'Capability' Brown arrived as gardener, to begin his own transformation of the landscape.

Lord Cobham dedicated his new temple, designed by James Gibbs, 'to the Liberty of our Ancestors', for which the Gothic style was deemed appropriate. Inside, the rooms are all circular, with moulded stone pilasters and plaster vaults – the main vault of the central space being gorgeously painted with heraldry. To be on the first floor gallery is an important architectural experience; and at the top of the staircase there is a belvedere with stone seats and a fine view over this former demesne of Lord Cobham and his successors, of which the National Trust is now guardian.

Stowe School gave us a long lease of the temple in 1970. It does have modern conveniences, if in rather surprising places, but the heating has to work hard to be noticed. We hope that the splendour of the temple and its surroundings will compensate those who stay here – it is one of the finest landscape gardens in the world.

From the logbook
*The sheer awesomeness of actually living in this place.*

*… we are spoiled for the future. Surely nowhere in Britain has a view like this.*

For up to 4 people
Parking adjacent

Spiral staircase
Dogs allowed

Ground floor

First floor

N ←

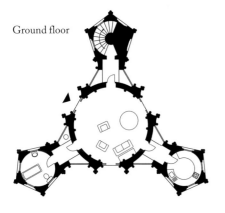

# The Grammar School

Kirby Hill, North Yorkshire

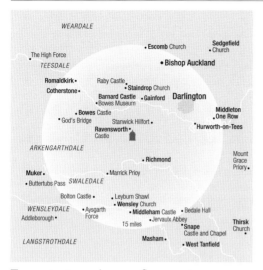

For up to 4 people
Open fire
Parking nearby

Steep staircase
Dogs allowed

Built in the discouraging reign of Queen Mary, this is one of a group of stone-roofed buildings that surround the large and airy village green of Kirby Hill. The Trust that owns the school was founded by Dr Dakyn on 11 May 1556. After Mass he explained to a numerous congregation how the Wardens of the Trust were to be chosen. On the feast of the Decollation of St John the names of six respectable parishioners were to be written on slips of paper and enclosed in balls of wax. These were to be put into a jar of water. Two names were then to be drawn and the jar of water with the remaining names put away in a cupboard, which he also provided. If a vacancy occurred during the year, a further ball of wax was to be drawn from the jar and opened. This is still done, and the jar is still kept in his cupboard, a very handsome one.

In 1957, after a life of 401 years, his school was closed, and in 1973 the Trustees gave us a long lease of it. We repaired the ground-floor schoolroom for use as a village hall, and the Tudor lodging of the master, upstairs, we turned into a flat. It has one particularly fine bedroom, looking into the churchyard, with views over the surrounding countryside, the village living up to its name. There is a large library of old school books (in the building when we arrived) and a general atmosphere of ancient peace, abetted by the church clock with its tranquillising strike.

From the logbook
*To quote Pevsner, 'a perfect and exceptional village'.*

*We have now slept in over 30 Landmarks, but the Grammar School remains our most favourite.*

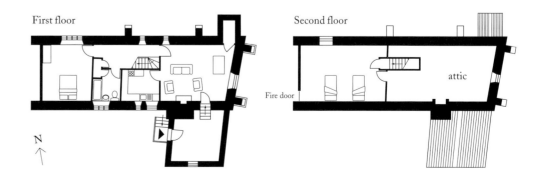

First floor

Second floor

attic

Fire door

N

# The Grange

Ramsgate, Kent

For up to 8 people
Open Fire
Enclosed garden
Adjacent parking

Augustus Pugin came to Ramsgate in 1843, in search of 'the delight of the sea with catholic architecture & a Library.' Here he built St Augustine's Grange, to live out his ideal of life in the Middle Ages in a family home nestling in the shadow of a benevolent monastery next door, completed by his son Edward and still thriving today.

The Grange reflects Pugin's belief in the Gothic style as the only true Christian architecture (he was a fervent convert to Catholicism). Here in his library, surrounded and sometimes interrupted by his large family, Pugin produced much of his finest work, working at prodigious speed as designs for the House of Lords and the Mediaeval Court at the Great Exhibition flowed effortlessly from his pen. He reserved some his finest flourishes for his own home: some remain, others we have reinstated. The house has a private chapel and a tower, from whose roof Pugin trained his telescope on ships in distress (today's Landmarkers can also climb out to watch more modern shipping from the freight ferry terminal, visible from the first floor and above).

The Grange remained in the Pugin family until 1928, when it became a school under the monks' care. Requisitioned during the war,

decline and then decay became inevitable, reaching crisis in 1996 when the house came on the market with permission to convert it into flats. It was too important for this and we made a rare purchase on the open market. We have returned most of the house to an appearance that Pugin himself would recognise, including the intricate, jewel-bright interiors (the north courtyard and a bedroom are presented as left by Edward Pugin, who lived at The Grange after his father's death).

Today, the house has regained the glowing vitality it enjoyed in the lifetime of its brilliant and mercurial designer. It offers a unique chance to step into the colourful and idiosyncratic world Augustus Pugin created for himself: to share the same merriment in the panelled dining room; to sit, as he did, in the library, surrounded by walls painted with the names of his favourite people and places.

*The Grange will be available for booking during 2006, please contact the Booking Office for further information.*

*Parts of the ground floor will be open to the public by appointment only on Wednesday afternoons.*

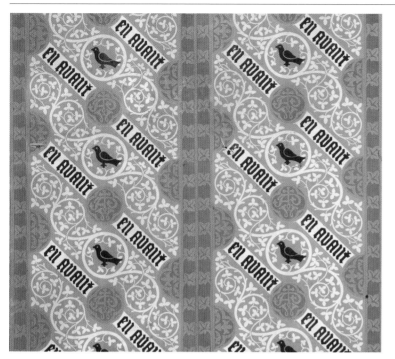

Photographs of The Grange before restoration

Ground floor

Chapel

First floor

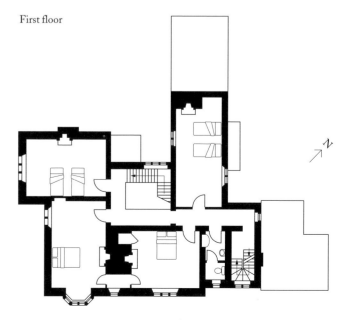

# Gurney Manor

Cannington, Somerset

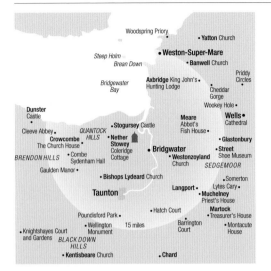

For up to 9 people
Open fire

Enclosed garden
Dogs allowed

When we first saw Gurney Manor it was divided into seven run-down flats. It is mainly late medieval, built, unusually, round a courtyard. Apart from the hall roof, which was renewed in about 1900, and Tudor windows and fireplaces in the adjoining solar block, the best medieval work survives unaltered, including a tiny oratory and a pentice, or covered passage, across the yard.

The man responsible for this was, as often, a lawyer, William Dodisham, son of a Gurney daughter. His heirs, the Mitchells, faded out before the Civil War and life thereafter as a tenant farm kept the house from major rebuilding. In the 1940s it was bought by a local developer, who divided it up into flats.

We have returned the house itself to its original undivided state. Its repair took eight years, carried out under the careful eye of our foreman, Philip Ford. New roof trusses were made in the traditional way, from oak shaped with an adze. The walls are rendered with lime plaster, buttered to a thinness equal to that achieved by medieval craftsmen.

The medieval house in its final and most fully developed form, with its balance of private and communal rooms, was a comfortable and convenient one. There can be few better ways of learning this than by staying here, in this tranquil and enclosed place. Cannington is a pleasant town not far from the Quantocks, with an excellent nursery garden.

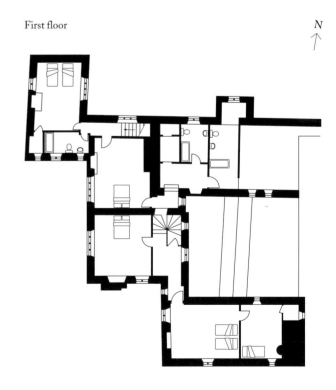

Ground floor

First floor

Pentice

Oratory

Old Kitchen

# Hampton Court Palace

East Molesey, Surrey

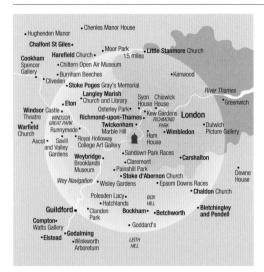

2 houses, one for 6 and one for 8.

Hampton Court Palace is no empty museum, but a large and thriving community, following a tradition set by George III, who allowed loyal servants to live here by Grace and Favour. Now home mainly to institutions and only a few residents, the sense of a secret life beyond the public eye survives – of doors leading to invisible corridors, of figures disappearing up a staircase with briefcase or shopping basket.

The opportunity we offer our visitors, on behalf of Historic Royal Palaces, is to become part of this life, to go past the security barrier, to make yourself at home in a palace. Hampton Court is so much a part of our history that it needs no new introduction. The details are best learned there, slowly and at first hand: our visitors are free to explore the gardens and most of the courtyards at all times, early and late, and the public rooms of the palace during opening hours.

Hampton Court has always been loved. Ernest Law, its chief historian, wrote, 'There is something so essentially homelike in the old Palace, that very few can dwell within it long, without growing attached to it'. Alexander Pope, visiting in 1718, was entranced: 'No lone house in Wales is more contemplative than Hampton Court. I walked there the other day by the moon, and met no creature of quality but the King, who was giving audience all alone to the birds under the garden wall'.

Fish Court and The Georgian House are in the middle on the left of the photograph. Whichever you choose, central London is only 35 minutes away by train.

# Fish Court

This apartment has its front door in Fish Court. It was originally for the Officers of the Pastry and lies in the service wing of the Tudor palace. Begun by Cardinal Wolsey, this was enlarged by Henry VIII, who entertained even more lavishly and added new kitchens, one entirely for the baking of pies. The windows look south over Master Carpenter's Court and north towards Bushey Park.

For up to 6 people
Parking nearby
Use of public gardens

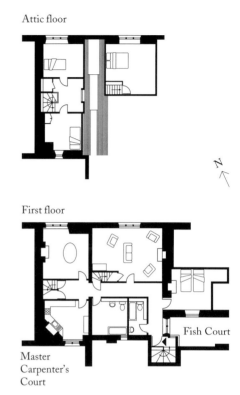

Attic floor

First floor

Fish Court

Master
Carpenter's
Court

# The Georgian House

The alternative is to stay in The Georgian House, an imposing building just north of the palace. It looks like a garrison commander's house, but was in fact a kitchen built in 1719 for George, Prince of Wales. Its near-twin at St James's Palace is thought to be by Vanbrugh. Later it became two houses, for the Clerk of Works and the Gardener. You can stay in the eastern one, with a private walled garden into which the morning sun shines. The main rooms are handsome, the attics have a fine view of the palace roofs, and in the kitchen is a huge blocked arch, once a royal cooking hearth.

For up to 8 people
Enclosed garden
Parking nearby

There are a twin bedroom, a single bedroom and a bathroom on the second floor.

First floor

Ground floor

Door to cloakroom

# The Hill House

Helensburgh, near Glasgow

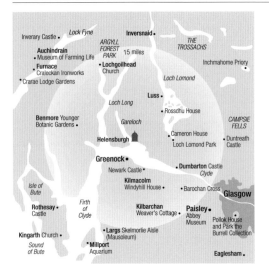

For up to 6 people     Parking nearby
Enclosed garden       Steep spiral staircase

The Hill House is the domestic masterpiece of the great Scottish architect Charles Rennie Mackintosh. Not particularly successful or lucky, he was an undoubted genius, a product of the flowering of art in Glasgow at the end of the nineteenth century. His influence is still discernible in many buildings and artefacts today. In 1902 he was commissioned by Walter Blackie, the publisher, to design this house for him and everything in it, a bold decision indeed.

The house (and the British public) has since been very lucky. With much of its original contents, it is now cared for by the National Trust for Scotland. In 1978 we came to the aid of the previous owner, the Royal Incorporation of Architects in Scotland. Bravely departing from its usual role as a professional body, it had in 1972 raised the money to buy the house when no other preservation body would take it on, but had scarce means to maintain it. As well as helping the RIAS directly, we took a lease of the top floor, which had been turned into a flat, and here we remain as tenants.

The principal room of our flat was the schoolroom of the Blackie family. Like all rooms once the domain of children, it has the feeling of a place where much spirit and energy have been expended. It is large and irregularly shaped, under the roof, with bookcases (now filled by us with Blackie's Annuals) and toy cupboards designed by Mackintosh – and with a large three-sided bay window, flooded with daylight, looking over the Firth of Clyde and beyond.

For those who admire Mackintosh or who wish to find out why others do so, to stay here is a privilege and experience without compare. The NTS usually opens the house between Easter and October. If the house is open, you have free access to it during opening hours, and normally to the garden at all times.

Helensburgh, on the upper edge of which The Hill House stands, is a pleasant, interesting place. An early and far-sighted example of town-planning, it was laid out on very generous lines in 1775. Big houses in big gardens line its broad tree-planted roads. And over the top of the hill the road leads down to Loch Lomond.

Top floor

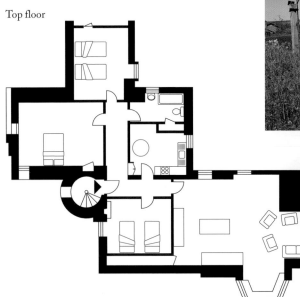

The Landmark apartment is on the top floor to the right of the photograph

# Hole Cottage

Cowden, Kent

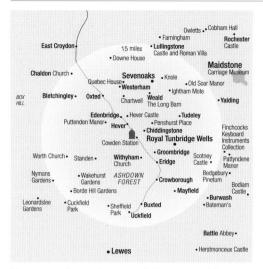

This is the cross-wing of a late medieval timber-framed hall-house, of high quality, the rest of which was pulled down in 1833. It lies by a small stream in a woodland clearing and, curiously enough, is easily accessible by railway, since it is only a 15 minute walk through the wood from Cowden station.

The Hole still has the true feeling of the Weald and of the deep woods in whose drip and shade the forges and furnaces of the Sussex ironmasters were established. This Wealden scene persists despite the great storm of October 1987. The logbook records the events of that night as the wind gathered strength: 'At about 3.30 we decided to go down to the sitting-room. As we sat with our one candle burning we heard a terrific crash in the big room upstairs: a big tree had fallen right on the peak of the roof. As the night went on trees fell one after another all about the house ... Mr Dale arrived with a flask of hot water at about 8.30 and a very welcome sight he was'. New trees are growing up fast, to enclose once again this solitary place, where you may enjoy a sleepy fire, the smell of its smoke and the sound of the stream.

From the logbook

*It's all green, and suddenly the cottage is standing there as it has been all the time.*

*To be woken up by birdsong and to be able to sit outside in the sun surrounded by bluebell woods is wonderful.*

For up to 4 people
Open fire
Garden

Adjacent parking
Uneven track
Dogs allowed

First floor

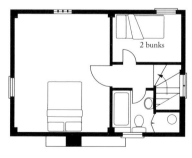

2 bunks

Ground floor

# Houghton West Lodge

Houghton, Norfolk

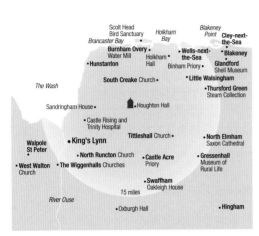

For up to 2 people
Open fire

Garden
Adjacent parking

This is one of four lodges guarding the approaches to Houghton Hall, Sir Robert Walpole's splendid rural palace. However, neither this, nor the similar North and East Lodges, formed part of the architectural and landscape improvements to which our first Prime Minister devoted so much energy and care. The work of Repton or Loudon, rather than Palladio, provided the model for their design, because they were not built until the 1840s. Sensibly, these new lodges made no attempt to rival the great house; they are entirely correct for a secondary entrance to the park, but pretend to nothing more.

Houghton West Lodge is small and neat, built around a central chimney, with a little yard and wash-house at the back, and large windows looking out into the surrounding woods. It stands by a drive that is now only a grassy track, set back from a country road. The last inhabitant left it some years ago, and the estate, having no further need of it, leased it to us.

This northern part of Norfolk has the character of a peninsula: the bright light, the sense of the sea not far away, the remoteness, the fearless and prolific wildlife. At the same time, the countryside for many miles around bears the stamp of civilised owners over several centuries. The opportunity to stay so agreeably at a nobleman's gate is not one to be missed.

From the logbook
*Such a variety of coastal scenery with a short distance, and so many delightful villages to visit.*

*Do read the logbook – it quickly yields enough to do in three weeks or more.*

Courtyard

# The House of Correction

Folkingham, Lincolnshire

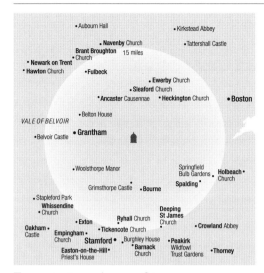

For up to 4 people
Open fire
Moated garden
Adjacent parking

Steep narrow
staircase
Dogs allowed

Folkingham is one of those agreeable places that are less important than they used to be. It has a single very wide street, lined on each side by handsome buildings, with a large eighteenth-century inn across the top end. Behind the houses, to the east, lie the moat and earthworks of a big medieval castle.

The House of Correction occupies the site of this castle. These minor prisons were originally intended for minor offenders – the idle (regarded as subversive) and the disorderly. Folkingham had a house of correction by 1611, replaced in 1808 by a new one built inside the castle moat and intended to serve the whole of Kesteven. This was enlarged in 1825 and given a grand new entrance. In 1878 the prison was closed and the inner buildings converted into ten dwellings, all demolished in 1955.

The grand entrance alone survives. It was designed by Bryan Browning, an original and scholarly Lincolnshire architect also

responsible for the Sessions House at Bourne. It is a bold and monumental work, borrowing from the styles of Vanbrugh, Sanmichele and Ledoux. Apart from cowing the malefactor it was intended to house the turnkey, and the Governor's horses and carriage. Now it gives entrance only to a moated expanse of grass – a noble piece of architecture in a beautiful and interesting place.

From the logbook
*Anyone who doesn't love their stay here needs to be locked up.*

*… the children were particularly taken with the handcuffs.*

*An all-too-short sentence.*

*What a pleasure to be an inmate!*

*How charming to find, behind the grand portico, something so elegant and snug.*

N
↑

Ground floor

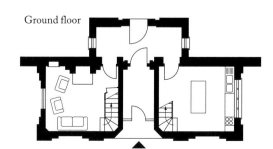

First floor

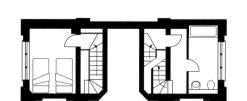

Attic

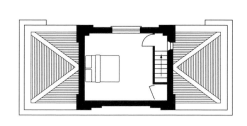

# Howthwaite

Grasmere, Cumbria

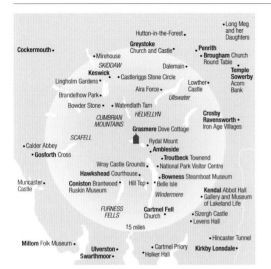

For up to 7 people
Open fire
Large wild garden
Parking nearby

Dogs allowed
Steep steps from
parking area

The land on which this house stands is immediately behind and above Dove Cottage. Wordsworth used to walk and sit here composing his poems, as his sister Dorothy records in her diary. For that reason, when it was offered for sale, the Trustees of Dove Cottage were anxious that it should fall into friendly hands and asked if we would join with them in buying it.

The house was built in 1926 by Miss Jessie Macdougall, of the family of millers, who bought the land from the widow of the famous Warden Spooner of New College. It seemed to us a good unaltered example of the solid houses put up by those cultivated, well-to-do people who were attracted to the Lake District; the kind of people who, among other things, had prompted the foundation of the National Trust. Certainly its light airy rooms and fine outlook and surroundings will give pleasure to many, particularly those who enjoy Wordsworth and the landscape that inspired him, whether to walk in or simply to look at.

From the logbook
*Spectacular views, spectacular house. What more could one (or seven people) ask?*

*We saw a red squirrel and two young deer. The children thought the garden was wonderful for exploring.*

*So many places to visit, and the house and garden so spacious, a happy place to which to return at the end of the day.*

*The driveway to the house is accessible in summer only.*

Ground floor

Terrace

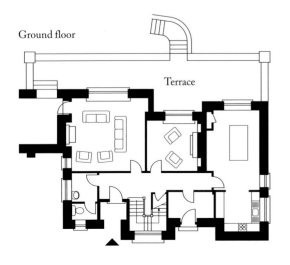

First floor

N

# Ingestre Pavilion

Tixall, Staffordshire

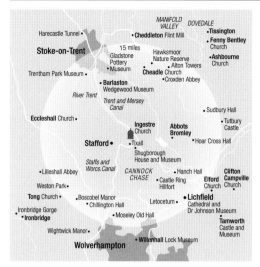

For up to 6 people
Open fire
Garden

Adjacent parking
Dogs allowed

The approach to this building is now from the side along a forest ride, but the long vista from it, between plantations to the Trent, is as it was when 'Capability' Brown drew up a scheme for 'an Intended Lawn' at Ingestre for the 2nd Viscount Chetwynd in 1756. The Pavilion was already there by then, added in about 1752 to an earlier, more formal layout.

The façade is a powerful and distinguished one. Curiously, for nearly two centuries it has been little more than that: by 1802 the building behind it, which the foundations show to have been surprisingly large and grand, had been demolished. In its place there are now new rooms designed by Philip Jebb, including a central octagonal saloon.

A local mason-architect named Charles Trubshaw (who trained as a sculptor under Scheemakers) worked at Ingestre around 1750. He probably put up the Pavilion, although it is unlikely that he was also its designer, able though he was. The Chetwynds, and after them the Talbots, were enlightened patrons of architecture – the parish church is by Wren – and undoubtedly this is the work of one of the best architects available.

From the logbook
*Fabulous walks all within a five-mile drive.*

*Evenings spent by a roaring fire, with jigsaws.*

*Our walk to Tixall yielded the biggest bunches of elderberries imaginable, from which we brewed our own cordial.*

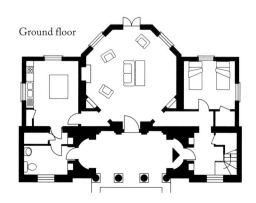

Ground floor

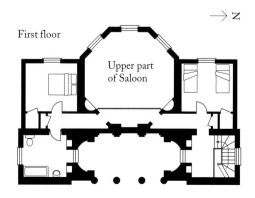

First floor

Upper part of Saloon

→ N

# Iron Bridge House

Ironbridge, Shropshire

For up to 4 people
Open fire

Parking nearby
for 1 car

The sale particulars said: 'These premises have been occupied by the Firm of Messrs Egerton Smith & Sons for many years. They were specially built, at a great cost, by the late Mr Smith and occupy a Unique Position in Ironbridge.' They certainly do – unique in the world, overlooking that harbinger of our age, forerunner and survivor, the Iron Bridge.

This building is the complete establishment of a substantial grocer, with a large house over a double-fronted shop, and all the offices behind, from storerooms to stables. From the cellars a tunnel runs to the bank of the River Severn, up which, until the late nineteenth century, the cargoes were brought by barge.

The shop is let to the Ironbridge Gorge Museum Trust. On the top two floors is where you can stay. The living-room has a fine iron fireplace cast here in Coalbrookdale, and this and every other room face the river, the bridge and the steep woods beyond. It is a wonderful place to be, with coal smoke drifting against the trees, and the sun glittering on the rather muddy Severn as it flows inexhaustibly beneath Abraham Darby's iron arch. All around, in Coalport, Ironbridge and Coalbrookdale, are the remains of industry's beginning.

From the logbook
*We knew we were going to be close to the bridge but we were presently surprised to find we were right next door. The views from the house are superb and because you are so far up you can people watch all day without being seen.*

First floor

Second floor

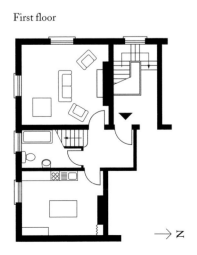

Fire Door

→ z

# Kingswear Castle

Near Dartmouth, Devon

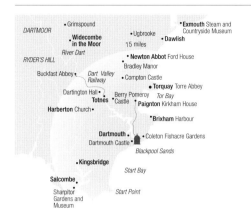

For up to 6 people
Garden
Roof platform
Parking nearby
Steep steps and staircases
Dogs allowed

In 1481 a new castle was begun at Dartmouth, to defend the harbour there. To support it from the opposite shore, Kingswear Castle was completed in 1502. Together they represent the most advanced military design of their day. For the first time large guns, such as murderers and serpyntynes, were mounted inside on the ground floor, with rectangular ports through which to fire them.

Within 50 years Kingswear Castle was redundant; for another century it was manned in time of war, but thereafter was left to decay, until rescued and turned into a summer residence in 1855 by a rich young bachelor, Charles Seale Hayne. During the last World War, a concrete blockhouse (now a thrilling, but spartan, extra bedroom), was built 50 yards from it.

We have restored the castle's ground floor to look as it did in 1502, with the living quarters above. The rooms have that sense of sturdy habitability in an exposed place, which the Victorians knew so well how to achieve, despite the building's inherent susceptibility to damp and cold (not even twenty-first century devices can fully overcome this). The tower stands almost on the water's edge (those with children beware) and its rooms are filled with shifting reflected light. From the windows you can look across to Dartmouth; or down the rocky coast, with its woods of maritime pine, and out to sea. Above all you can watch the river, busy now with friendly shipping.

From the logbook
*The only trouble with this castle is that it is so hard to leave it to do any sightseeing and utterly miserable to leave it to go home.*

*I would like to spend all night on the battlements watching the stars.*

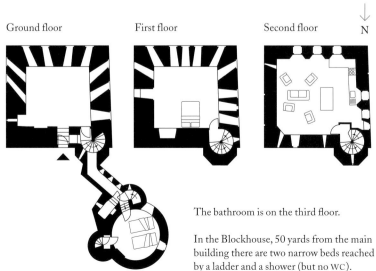

Ground floor    First floor    Second floor    N

The bathroom is on the third floor.

In the Blockhouse, 50 yards from the main building there are two narrow beds reached by a ladder and a shower (but no WC).

# Knowle Hill

Near Ticknall, Derbyshire

For up to 5 people
Solid fuel stove
Long gated access track

Enclosed garden
Steep steps outside
Dogs allowed

In 1698 Walter Burdett, a younger son born nearby at Foremark, retired from the Middle Temple. On land leased from his friend, Thomas Coke of Melbourne, he built for himself a most curious house on the side of a ravine. Here, being a likeable and sociable person, he entertained his many friends; and around it he formed a garden which, for all its formal structure of terraces and pools, blended evocatively with the natural landscape – remarkably so at that early date.

In the 1760s the house was pulled down by Walter's great-nephew, but the atmosphere of a woodland retreat was preserved – and so was a tunnel leading to a mysterious rock-cut chamber from the cellars. A Gothick summerhouse, which soars like a ruined castle on the valley's edge, was built on an upper terrace, with a cottage for a custodian behind. Until abandoned in the twentieth century, parties came often to walk here amid the picturesque delights of trees and water. Picturesque it still is, but parents will want to keep a close eye on small children because of steep drops and the stream in the ravine below.

By 1989 Knowle Hill was divided between three owners. Its remote position down a long gated farm track deterred most would-be rescuers, but it is now reunited, and the quiet process of revival is under way.

We have repaired the cottage for you to stay in, with the summerhouse as your drawing-room. It opens on to a sunny lawn, with a view into the woods beyond and, if you are lucky, a glimpse of water tumbling over a cascade.

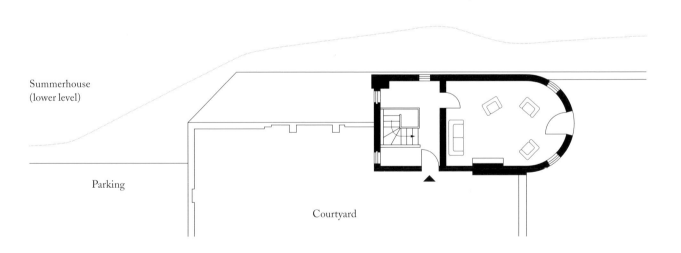

Summerhouse
(lower level)

Parking

Courtyard

Cottage
(upper level)

Additional WC below
at courtyard level

N ←

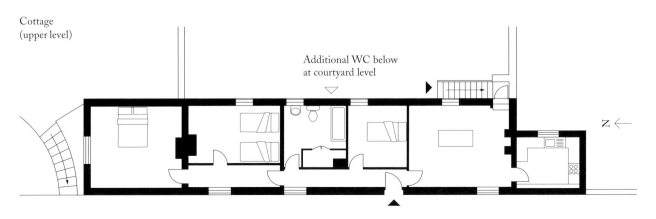

# Langley Gatehouse

Near Acton Burnell, Shropshire

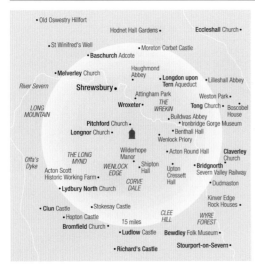

For up to 6 people
Solid fuel stove
Enclosed garden

Parking nearby
Dogs allowed

Like all the best buildings this one is hard to find. To add confusion, its two faces are each quite different: one, formerly presented to the outside world but now looking on to a working farm, is of plain dressed stone. The other, which once looked inwards at Langley Hall (demolished by 1880), is timber-framed in the best local tradition. Both are Jacobean, although the lower part of the outer wall was already ancient when Sir Humphrey Lee added this gatehouse above it in about 1610.

The new building was probably for the Steward, or important guests. The parlour, over the gate passage, was panelled (and is again) with a moulded plaster cornice. On either side are rooms of generous size, and above are attics, squeezed in among the aisled structure of the queen-post roof. The roof slates of moss-covered Harnage stone are thick with fossilised shells.

The gatehouse was near to collapse when, as a joint operation with English Heritage, we began work on it in 1992 – indeed its north-east corner post appeared to be supported solely by a wine bottle wedged beneath its decayed foot. The exemplary quality of the repairs is a pleasure to see; as also is the view from the main windows down a wide valley to the Wrekin.

From the logbook
*We loved being so close to the farm – tractors and cattle sounds reminding us we were away from home!*

Ground floor

First floor

Second floor

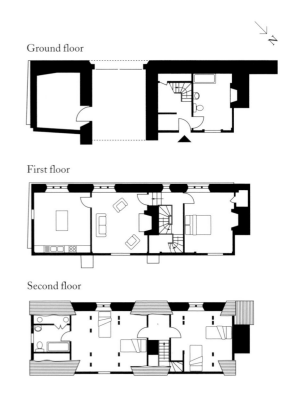

# Laughton Place

Near Lewes, East Sussex

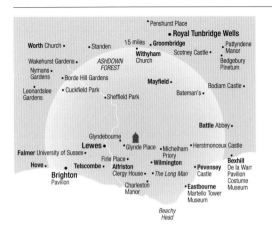

For up to 4 people
Moated garden
Roof platform
Parking nearby

Steep spiral staircase
Dogs allowed

This building has an illustrious pedigree, which it wears with the lonely and battered dignity of a nobleman fallen on hard times. From about 1400, Laughton was the chief manor of the Pelhams, without whom eastern Sussex would not have been as it is. In 1534 Sir William, who had attended his king at the Field of the Cloth of Gold, remodelled the house on a grand scale, round a moated courtyard and with terracotta decoration in the newest Renaissance fashion. All that has survived is this bold brick tower, which stood close to the main hall, an outlook post and set of secure private rooms combined. By 1600 the family had abandoned Laughton, driven by the damp (a problem still, on which we are working) to build again on higher ground, and slowly the house decayed.

Then, in 1753, Henry Pelham, politician and brother to the splendid Duke of Newcastle, had the idea of surrounding the tower with a new Gothick farmhouse. The result was very charming, with a pediment between crenellated side-wings, and pointed windows. Thus it continued until sold by the Pelhams in 1927. The new owner pulled down the wings, leaving only the tower. It stands, with a couple of other buildings, within the wide circle of the Downs, down a long drive.

When we bought it in 1978, the tower had great cracks in its sides, and the floors had fallen in – much engineering and lime mortar went into its repair. The rooms inside are plain, apart from the delicate arabesque decoration of the terracotta windows, the moulded terracotta doors and the Pelham Buckle, the badge won by prowess in the Middle Ages and used as a family emblem ever since. The building, if long neglected, was obviously once something to be proud of.

Ground floor

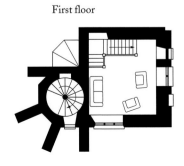
First floor

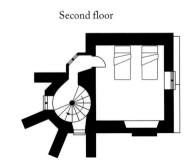
Second floor

Third floor

N

# Lettaford

North Bovey, Devon

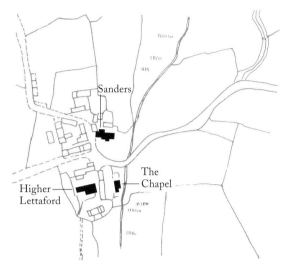

One house for 7, one for 5 and a former chapel for 2.

The fringes of Dartmoor gave a surprisingly good living to those who had the tenacity to carry on in its sometimes harsh climate, grazing their cattle on the rough upland pasture, cultivating crops in the tiny fields lower down. Throughout the Middle Ages they maintained their own way of life and their own economy, carefully adapted to suit their surroundings and best seen now in the longhouses in which they chose to live, found nowhere else in such numbers in the comfortable South West of England. It is in the building of these on a grander scale, with fine masonry and even carved ornament, that we see evidence of renewed activity from 1500 on, when a growth of population and prosperity in Devon as a whole led to new buildings and new settlements.

Lettaford is an old settlement, men having lived here from before 1300. The public road that leads to it breaks up into tracks, taking you on to the moor itself; and all its three farmhouses are, in origin at least, sixteenth-century longhouses. It is sited in a hollow for shelter, its buildings grouped around a green, including a former Methodist chapel, the only one not related directly to farming. It is like many other, similar hamlets but few remain so secret or complete. The self-contained resourceful life of an upland people goes on around you as it always has; and the world contracts to Dartmoor's limits, beyond which only the adventurous go.

# Lettaford

## The Chapel

The Chapel is a plain granite building typical of rural Nonconformity, built by Miss Pynsent of Higher Lettaford in 1866. Firstly Bible Christian, and later Methodist, it closed in 1978. With little chance of survival on its own, its loss would have been a pity for Lettaford, so we took it on. Here two of you can cook, eat and sleep all in one big room, with an open fire, tucked away at the edge of the green beside a small stream.

For up to 2 people
Open fire
Parking nearby
Dogs allowed

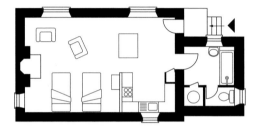

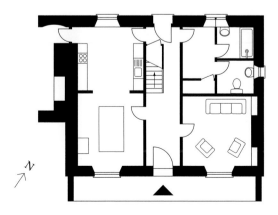

Ground floor

## Higher Lettaford

Higher Lettaford had been empty for some years when we bought it in 1987. It was once a longhouse, but in about 1840 its lower end was rebuilt, most comfortably, by two Misses Pynsent, who may have run a small Nonconformist school here.

Their house has large windows, and a verandah, introducing a whiff of Torquay and a life of seaside ease to this hard-working place. The bedrooms are some of the prettiest in any Landmark, and from the front door, the old track leads up to the moor.

For up to 7 people
Open fire
Garden
Parking nearby
Dogs allowed

Ground floor

First floor

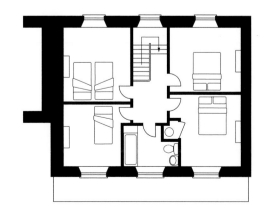

# Sanders

Sanders is a near perfect Dartmoor long-house of about 1500, arranged on the usual plan of inner room, hall, cross-passage and shippon, all under one roof, with a shouldered porch originally the entrance for both cows and people. The walls are made of blocks of granite ashlar, some of them enormous. This was a house of high quality, but it declined into a labourer's cottage long enough ago to avoid damaging improvements.

For up to 5 people
Open fire
Garden
Parking nearby
Steep staircase
Dogs allowed

From the logbook
*Wonderful house, lovely walks – heard cuckoos, saw tiny new born foals and a beautiful array of wild flowers.*

Ground floor

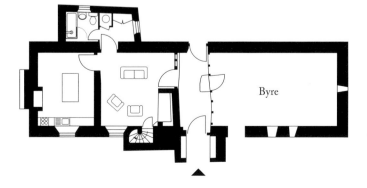

Byre

First floor

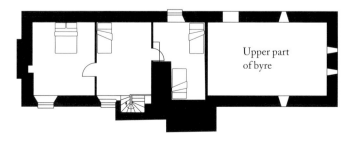

Upper part of byre

N

# The Library

Stevenstone, near Great Torrington, Devon

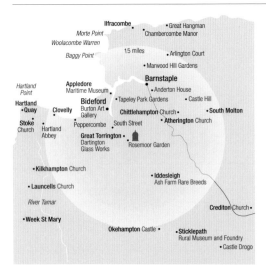

For up to 4 people
Open fire
Enclosed garden

Parking nearby
Steep narrow spiral
staircase

The Library, and its smaller companion the Orangery, stand in well-mannered incongruity beside the ruins of Victorian Stevenstone, with the remains of a grand arboretum around them. Stevenstone was rebuilt by the very last of the Rolles in 1870, but these two pavilions survive from an earlier remodelling of 1710–20. The façade of the Library, with its giant order and modillion cornice, looks like the work of a lively, probably local, mason-architect, familiar with the work of such as Talman and Wren.

Why a library in the garden? It probably started life as a perfectly ordinary banqueting house and only assumed its more learned character later on. Why it should have done so is a mystery, of a pleasantly unimportant kind. By the time we first saw it, when it

came up for sale in 1978, the bookshelves had been dispersed and the Library had been a house for many years, the fine upper room divided and the loggia closed in, while the Orangery was about to collapse altogether. We put new roofs on both buildings and, on the Library, a new eaves cornice carved from 170 feet of yellow pine by a local craftsman, Richard Barnett. The loggia is open again, and the main room has returned to its full size. To stay in this particularly handsome building, even without the books, is an enlightening experience.

From the logbook
*What an exquisite building – who needs to go anywhere else?*

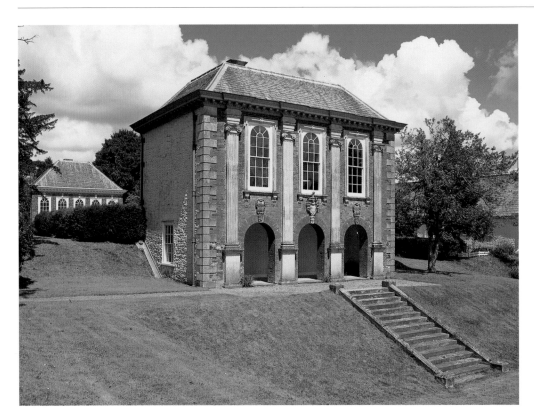

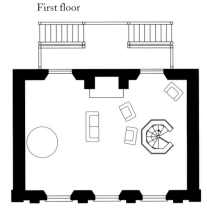

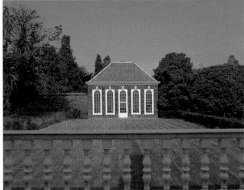

There are two beds (no bathroom) in the Orangery, which stands 100 ft from the main building. It is unheated and therefore we do not recommend it for winter use.

Ground floor

First floor

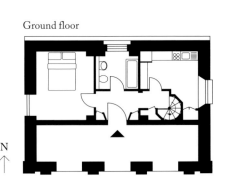

N
↑

# Lock Cottage

Stoke Pound, Worcestershire

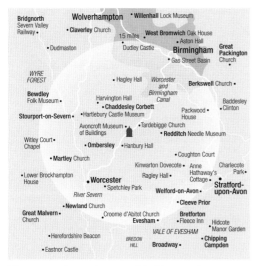

For up to 4 people
Open fire
Small enclosed yard

Parking a short
walk away

We hope that this lock cottage will give you a taste for travel by canal, which is the prime way to see England at walking pace without actually having to walk. Until the 1950s many such handsome unpretentious buildings served and graced our canal system; but they were demolished ruthlessly. Indeed it was, in particular, the destruction of Thomas Telford's Junction House at Hurlestone on the Shropshire Union canal which maddened us into starting the Landmark Trust.

This survivor lies on the Worcester & Birmingham canal, built between 1790 and 1815, which runs for 30 miles from Diglis Basin in Worcester to Gas Street in Birmingham.

Birmingham, as boaters all discover, is on a hill, and it takes 58 locks in 16 miles to lift this canal from the Severn to the Birmingham level. Of these locks, 30 are here at Tardebigge, the longest flight in Britain.

Our cottage is between locks 31 and 32, by bridge 49, a bridge as beautiful as all the others (which you must cross after leaving your car to reach the towpath and the cottage); canals are a wonderful demonstration that beauty and utility can be combined. Alas today only pleasure boats and towpath walkers will pass in front of your windows, but at the lock, you may well be offered a lift up the flight; and at the top, with its surprising view, you will, if you possess any spirit at all, decide to navigate one day still further, through the tunnel under the green hill beyond.

From the logbook
*Sitting in the cottage with a cup of tea and watching the boats go by is infinitely preferable to jumping on and off a boat watching the cottages go by.*

Ground floor

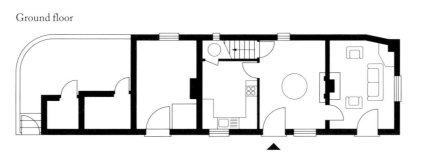

First floor

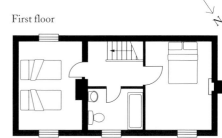

# Lower Porthmeor

Near Zennor, Cornwall

Lower Porthmeor is a township, or farm hamlet, typical of this area of West Penwith, where sometimes as many as four houses are grouped round a single farmyard. The houses are not themselves of great age, but they represent a tradition as old as the tiny stone-hedged fields in which they stand, fields that have scarcely changed since the Iron Age. With their pleasant sturdy buildings, such settlements can be seen dotted all along the green coastal shelf running west from St Ives, bounded on one side by a ridge of high moor, on the other by the Atlantic cliffs.

We bought the farm, which had been derelict for some years, in conjunction with the National Trust. There are two houses, separated by the farmyard, both facing south, and each with its own granite-walled garden. From their back doors, it is a short walk across fields to where a little valley cuts through the cliffs to form a rocky bay.

Two houses for 4 and one for 5.

# Arra Venton

Arra Venton, a house of somewhat mixed parentage, came on the market just after we had taken on Lower Porthmeor. There were once two buildings, a chapel and a smithy, on to one end of which a cottage was added early this century. Then, in 1952, the whole was joined together, in an eccentric if imaginative fashion. Altered again since then, and treated and painted in an unsympathetic way, it spoiled the elemental landscape of which it is part, and looked horrible from our other buildings. So we bought it, and de-improved it, to make it simple and unified again; and very pleasant it is.

For up to 5 people
Solid fuel stove
Garden
Adjacent parking
Dogs allowed

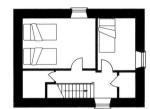

First floor

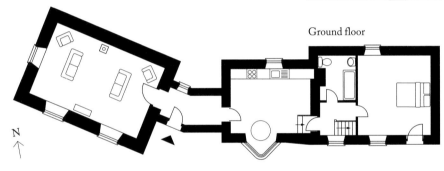

Ground floor

N
↑

# Lower Porthmeor

## The Captain's House

The Captain's House is simpler than its companion, The Farmhouse, and dates from the 1840s. It, too, has a massive kitchen fireplace and a snug parlour. There were once two houses, but the lower half was long ago given over to animals. This was the childhood home of Arthur Berryman, the last of the Lower Porthmeor Berrymans, who was both farmer and Captain in a local tin mine. His forebears settled here before 1600, and cousins still farm Higher Porthmeor.

For up to 4 people
Solid fuel stove
Enclosed garden
Adjacent parking
Dogs allowed

Ground floor

First floor

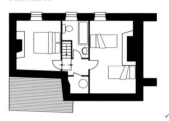

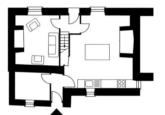

## The Farmhouse

The Farmhouse was built in about 1800 and has a handsome front of granite ashlar, paid for perhaps with money from the tin stamps nearby. Inside are further hints of wealth, in a bedroom with a dado and a pretty fireplace. But the great chimney piece in the kitchen has a granite monolith for its lintel, like many older houses in the area.

For up to 4 people
Solid fuel stove
Garden
Adjacent parking
Dogs allowed

Ground floor

First floor

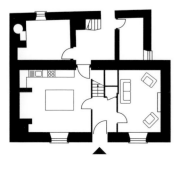

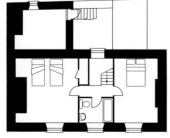

# Luttrell's Tower

Eaglehurst, Southampton, Hampshire

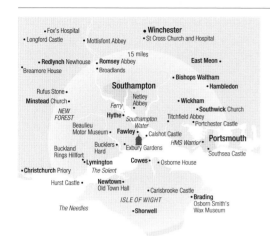

This is an exceptionally fine Georgian folly, possibly the only surviving work of Thomas Sandby, first Professor of Architecture at the Royal Academy. It stands on the shore of the Solent looking towards Cowes. The view, particularly of ships entering and leaving Southampton by the deep water channel, is magnificent – as, in another way, is the sight, from its top, of the Fawley refinery and power station. It also has the magic of those places where trees, especially yews and ilexes as here, come right down to the salt sea's edge.

It was built for Temple Luttrell, a Member of Parliament (but reputedly a smuggler here) who died in Paris in 1803. His brother-in-law, Lord Cavan, who commanded our forces in Egypt from 1801, was the next owner and brought with him the two mysterious feet on a plinth of Nubian granite, now at the tower and thought to be the base of a XIXth dynasty statue of Rameses II.

Thereafter the tower passed through various hands; Queen Victoria nearly bought it (with Eaglehurst House) instead of Osborne, and Marconi used it for his wireless experiments of 1912. Sir Clough Williams-Ellis designed the double staircase that gives access to it from the beach, too grand really for anyone but Neptune.

We bought the tower in 1968. Inside, all the rooms have fine chimney pieces, and the top room, a splendid eyrie, which we have arranged so that you can cook, eat and sit in it, is a fine plaster and shellwork as well. There is a tunnel from the basement to the beach, made perhaps for the smuggling Member.

For up to 4 people
Open fire
Adjacent parking

Spiral staircase
Dogs allowed

Second floor

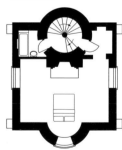

First floor

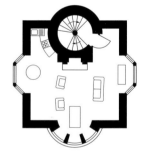

Ground floor

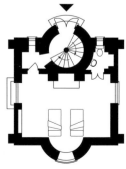

There is also a WC with a basin off the staircase on a mezzanine floor. There is a table tennis table in the basement.

# Lynch Lodge

Alwalton, near Peterborough, Cambridgeshire

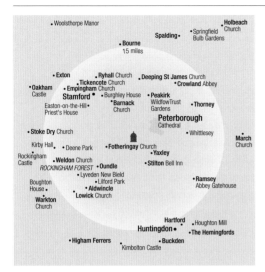

For up to 2 people
Open fire
Garden

Adjacent parking
Dogs allowed

Alwalton lies in the extreme north of the former county of Huntingdon, on the river Nene a few hundred yards from the Great North Road. Despite its nearness to poor overgrown Peterborough it has a quiet open village street, a cul de sac ending in a patch of green, on which stands the Lynch Lodge. This building is the fine, two-storey Jacobean porch from the Drydens' house at Chesterton, where the poet often stayed with his favourite cousin. It was brought here when the house was demolished in 1807 and erected as a lodge to Milton Park by the Fitzwilliam family, who had a dower-house in the village. The Lynch drive having been closed (not surprisingly as it was three miles long), it now presides over a farm entrance and a rough track to the river.

We were told about it by a neighbour and bought it from the Fitzwilliam estate. Never a very convenient dwelling, it had been altered and enlarged over the years to accommodate bigger families. We have restored it to its original form, with one small room up and one more generous room down, joined by a new staircase.

From the logbook
*The highlight of my week was seeing a kingfisher for the first time flying low across the river.*

*I really loved the simplicity and beauty of the furniture and decor, the spiral staircase – castle-like, gorgeous.*

*What an enchanting way to begin the Landmark experience.*

Ground floor

First floor

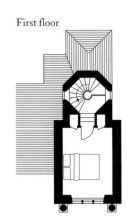

# The Mackintosh Building

Comrie, Perthshire

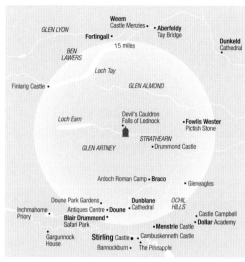

For up to 4 people     Enclosed garden
Open fire                Parking nearby

This building was designed by Charles Rennie Mackintosh and dates from 1903–4, a time when he was doing his very best work (see The Hill House). It was commissioned (at whose suggestion we know not) by a local draper and ironmonger, Peter Macpherson, as a shop with a flat above and workrooms in the attics. The flat passed into separate ownership some years ago, but we were able to reunite the two, by buying the flat in 1985, and then the shop as well, from Mr. Macpherson's granddaughter.

We have redecorated the flat, which has good and characteristic detail. The main room runs into the projecting turret, or tourelle, which Mackintosh added to the outer angle of the building in a nod towards Scottish Baronial architecture. This gives it an airy feel, and a pleasant view of the River Earn and the wooded hills beyond. At the back is a long garden, reached by a passage from the street.

Comrie is an unfussy highland town, with a bridge over a pebbly river, a whitewashed church and a small square, on the corner of which, right at the centre of things, stands this distinguished and surprising building.

From the logbook
*Magnificent countryside and enough to do and see to fill a lifetime.*

*It has made us quite determined to find out more about Charles Rennie Mackintosh.*

*We were especially fond of the bay window – looking out on to the world of Comrie.*

*The marriage of Mackintosh building to Landmark Trust is a truly happy one.*

First floor

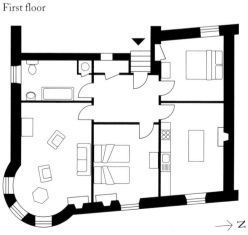

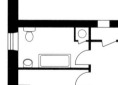

→ N

# Maesyronen Chapel

Near Hay-on-Wye, Powys

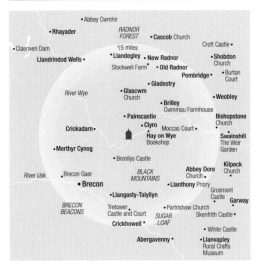

For up to 4 people
Open fire
Enclosed garden

Adjacent parking
Dogs allowed

Here we have taken on the neat and tiny cottage built before 1750 on to the end of one of Wales's shrines of Nonconformity, the Maesyronen chapel. The chapel itself, converted from a barn in 1696, dates from the early vernacular days when any suitable building was made use of for enthusiastic worship. Although officially founded just after the Act of Toleration, it had probably been used for secret meetings before that, which explains its isolated position. Its simple layout and furniture, added as and when the congregation could afford it, follows the basic pattern that prevailed for the next two centuries. It has high box-pews and a higher pulpit, lit from behind by a window, and all of a plainness that fully conveys the essentials of this new and radical rural faith.

The chapel, where services are still held, is cared for by Trustees, who asked for our help. By taking a lease on the cottage we hope we have given both buildings a future. Staying here, perched on a high shelf above the Wye (wrapped up warmly in winter), you can look out across the Black Mountains. Here you can sample a different and earlier kind of life from one that has tended to eclipse it in the public imagination, that which grew up around the chapels of the South Wales valleys in the nineteenth century.

From the logbook
*I want another week, no, a month, no – for ever!*

*The complete peace here has restored us and we'll be sorry to leave.*

*All objectives achieved. 1. good walking; 2. peace and quiet; 3. cosy cottage; 4. escape rat race.*

*Come to Maesyronen especially to 'do' the Hay bookshops.*

*We will miss the mountains tomorrow night.*

Ground floor

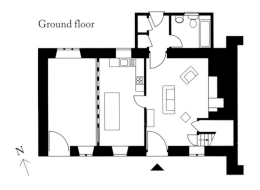

First floor

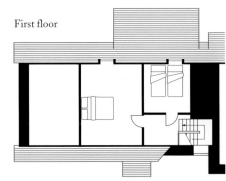

# Manor Farm

Pulham Market, near Diss, Norfolk

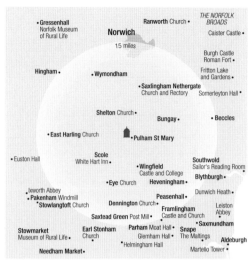

For up to 8 people
Open fire
Garden
Small moat nearby

Adjacent parking
Steep staircases
Dogs allowed

Manor Farm is a vernacular building, put up by men who had done the same job many times before and knew just what they were doing. It is mainly late Elizabethan and, apart from minor additions, has not been altered since. South Norfolk was then more thickly populated, and wooded, than today; Pulham was a thriving market town and there is no sign here that oak was in short supply. The yeoman farmer whose home it was added to his income with a bit of weaving – Pulham work, a furnishing fabric, was well-known. To judge by his house, he was quite comfortably off.

In the first half of the twentieth century a good living was more difficult to come by for a small farmer. Manor Farm decayed, and its vulnerable thatch and plaster disintegrated. The lavish oak partitions and moulded beams were nearly sold as antiques. But in 1948 it was recognised for what it was and rescued in the nick of time by Mr and Mrs Dance of the Society for the Protection of Ancient Buildings, who repaired it to the highest of William Morris's standards, and who later bequeathed Methwold Old Vicarage to the SPAB (now leased to us to be enjoyed as a Landmark).

30 years later, if Manor Farm was to continue as a permanent home, it would have needed a good deal of modernisation, which would not inevitably have been in its best interests. So in 1979 we took it on. The improvements we did decide to make were contained within an eighteenth-century addition, and any shortcomings in the heating seemed a small sacrifice for keeping the yeoman's house in all its rich simplicity.

Ground floor

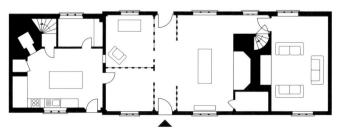

First floor

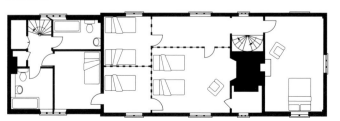

N

# Margells

Branscombe, Devon

For up to 5 people
Open fire
Garden

Parking nearby
Dogs allowed

From outside this is just a plain stone cottage, pleasant enough if unremarkable; but inside it is another matter. The broad passage running across the middle of the house has oak partitions on each side, and both the downstairs rooms have ceilings of heavily moulded oak beams. Upstairs the rooms are open to the roof, and a contemporary wall painting remains in one of them. The staircase has solid oak treads and all the doorways are of well-above-average quality. It is a very strong, interesting and well-preserved interior, dating from the end of the sixteenth century.

What is all this doing in so small a house and where, indeed, was the kitchen? The explanation may be that this was the parlour wing of a larger house, which was later divided into several cottages. Whatever the answer, the result is most satisfying.

Moreover, the surroundings are extremely pleasant. The group of old cottages, of which Margells is one, includes a distinctly agreeable pub. Near the house a stream of water comes out of a spout in the wall and flows away under the road. Opposite, over the roofs, a wood climbs up a hill, and beyond that is the sea.

From the logbook
*We have loved the fresh air and exercise and long evenings with the fire lit in a wonderful, warm, welcoming house.*

*Go and watch hang gliders on the cliffs straight out from the house.*

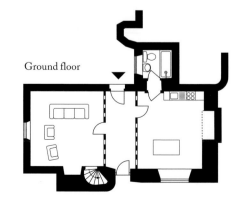

Ground floor

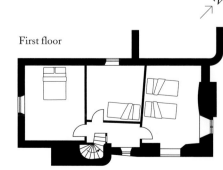

First floor

# Marshal Wade's House

Abbey Churchyard, Bath

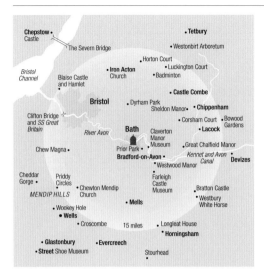

For up to 4 people
Access by narrow, steep stairs

No private parking
Gas coal fire

This is a sophisticated building of about 1720 in the very centre of the town. Once there were others like it, but they have gone, taking with them the reputation of good architects practising in Bath before the more famous Woods. They must have found a good patron in George Wade (made Field Marshal in 1744) who was the city's MP and whose London house was designed by Lord Burlington.

When we took it on in 1975, we first of all restored the windows and the shop front, and decluttered and restored the interiors. Later, we cleaned the front too, with sprinkled water and lime poultices to dissolve encrusted grime.

The second-floor rooms have good panelling, and all the windows look along the west front of the Abbey. From here, on a level with the angels, you can see the great carving of Jacob's ladder. There is also an exceptional view from the bathroom on the third floor, and from the bath.

All around there are more good things to see within walking distance than almost anywhere in Britain. Leave your car behind, come by train, live over the shop, just be in Bath.

From the logbook
*The nearest to Florence you get in England, with stunning views all the way to trees on the hills.*

*This is such a special Landmark; one of those that you can't believe you're actually allowed to stay in.*

*Everything within easy reach on foot – essential in Bath!*

*The Abbey Square was like an Italian piazza.*

*Living here is like having a box at the theatre.*

Second floor

Third floor

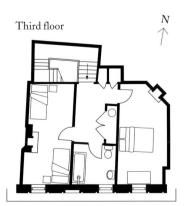

N

# Martello Tower

Aldeburgh, Suffolk

For up to 4 people
Solid fuel stove
Roof terrace

Parking nearby
Shower only
Dogs allowed

This is the largest and most northerly of the chain of towers put up by the Board of Ordnance to keep out Napoleon. Built in the shape of a quatrefoil for four heavy guns, nearly a million bricks were used in its construction. It stands at the root of the Orford Ness peninsula, between the River Alde and the sea, a few hundred yards from Aldeburgh. We bought it, sadly damaged, in 1971, with eight acres of saltings. We removed the derelict 1930s superstructure (once rather elegant, by Justin Vulliamy), repaired the outer brickwork and parapet (a tremendous job) and restored the vaulted interior, which has a floor of teak and an intriguing echo. The bedrooms are screened from the central living area but not fully divided, so that, lying in bed, you can still have a sense of being in a larger loftier space – and you can enjoy some conversation with your fellow guests.

Martello Towers were built to deter the French, not the elements, and inevitably, in this exposed position, some of the water finds its way inside. The installation of a purpose-made canopy over the main living space now provides significant protection. We do not expect it to be there forever, but for now it has an agreeable nautical resonance of sails and campaign tents. Here you may live with the sea, the wind and rain sometimes, the light at Orford Ness flashing at night, and Aldeburgh at just the right distance. The stone-flagged battery on the roof, with the mountings of guns and a high, thick parapet for shelter, is a very pleasant place to be. Amber and bloodstones, brought by glaciers from Scandinavia, have been found on the beach. Many visitors bring sailing dinghies.

Main floor

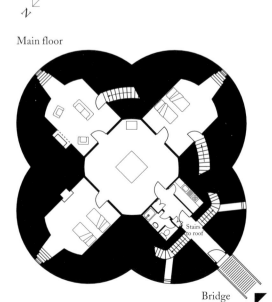

# Methwold Old Vicarage

Methwold, Norfolk

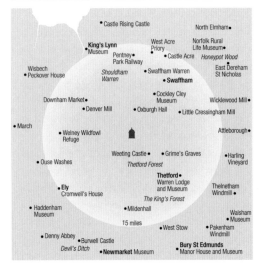

For up to 5 people
Open fire and solid
fuel stove

Enclosed garden
Adjacent parking
Dogs allowed

No vicar has lived in the Old Vicarage at Methwold for over two hundred years, but this is the least of the puzzles about this intriguing building. Externally, its chief glory is the late fifteenth century brick gable-end, whose octagonal stack seems a sampler of early Tudor patterns. This gable-end is unique in Norfolk and possibly beyond, and despite its modest village setting, bears comparison with the greatest early East Anglian brickwork such as that of Oxburgh and Layer Marney.

The jettied, timber-framed range behind the gable is also advanced for its day, the stout cruciform spine beams on both floors telling of a building designed to have two stories from the start. These beams are beautifully moulded and so too are the fireplace surrounds and bressumer. Upstairs acanthus leaves by the hand of a late sixteenth-century craftsman run rampant across stud and plasterwork.

The greatest puzzle is why such a richly decorated house should have been built for the priest of a village on the edge of the fens, famed only for its rabbits – but this need not trouble unduly those who come to take pleasure in its rarity. The Old Vicarage had been condemned for demolition when Monica and Harry Dance came to its rescue in 1964, and they eventually relinquished Manor Farm to Landmark in order to move to Methwold. The Dances later bequeathed the Old Vicarage to the Society for the Protection of Ancient Buildings, of which Monica was the renowned Secretary for many years and from whom we were happy to accept a long lease.

An engaging nineteenth-century vicar of Methwold, the Reverend Denny Gedge, bemoaned the dilapidated state of the Old Vicarage even in his own day (living himself in a 'neat new vicarage at the other end of the parish') and wailed 'Oh! if some charitable millionaire even now would buy it … its price would be very small.' We think he would have approved of today's solution.

First floor

Ground floor

# Monkton Old Hall

For up to 7 people
Open fire
Enclosed garden

Adjacent parking
Steep spiral staircase
Dogs allowed

Although much altered and rebuilt, the Old Hall has a strongly medieval character, a mixture of spareness and solidity. It dates from before 1400 and was probably the guest house of a small priory outside the walls of Pembroke. Just off the pilgrim route to St David's, and close to a great castle, the monks could expect to put up any number of people at unexpected times. Since then the house has been left to become ruinous at least twice, and then been rescued in the nick of time.

Its Victorian saviour was J. R. Cobb, a scholar and romantic who restored several castles in South Wales. In the 1930s it was discovered again, by Miss Muriel Thompson, another romantic. She repaired the house, with help from Clough Williams-Ellis, and created a garden, on a long and possibly ancient terrace cut out of the hillside. She wanted to share her home with others, to revive a monastic sense of hospitality: many people came to stay and her Christmas parties were famous. It was the memory of this and the appeal the Old Hall has, especially for children, that made Mrs Campbell, to whom it was left, think of passing it on to us.

We made the house slightly smaller by removing a decaying nineteenth-century wing, and moved a massive stone chimney piece from a bedroom to the hall. To improve this lofty and noble room further we painted its roof timbers a deep Pugin red. With this and the long vaulted undercroft beneath, an empty space for children to let off steam, and the large and interesting garden, with its old walls and grandstand view of Pembroke Castle, there is little temptation to go elsewhere. But should you wish to make your own pilgrimage to St David's, or explore the cliffs and castles of Pembrokeshire, or just go to the beach, the house will welcome you back, to warm yourself by the fire.

First floor

Ground floor

# Morpeth Castle

Morpeth, Northumberland

For up to 7 people    Adjacent parking
Solid fuel stove    Steep spiral staircase
Enclosed garden    Dogs allowed

The walls of a new castle in Morpeth were built soon after 1200, on a hill overlooking the River Wansbeck. Our gatehouse was added a century later, more for show than defence. Its builder, Lord Greystoke, wanted its presence felt, because this was to be a court-house, in which manorial justice was dispensed – an important function in the unruly Borders. The court was held in the large room on the first floor.

This room was divided by a screen, behind which the plaintiffs waited (its replacement hides nothing more dangerous than the kitchen). Between sittings the gatehouse served as a lodging, probably for the bailiff. These arrangements disappeared in later alterations, however, just before 1700 and again in 1860. Each time, a new house was formed inside the walls. We have tried to keep something of each but to make sense of the medieval layout as well.

In 1516 Margaret, sister of Henry VIII and widow of James IV of Scotland, stayed for four months in Morpeth Castle as she fled from her enemies in Scotland and sought refuge with her brother. The one great military event in the castle's history was in 1644 when a garrison of 500 Lowland Scots held it for Parliament for 20 days against 2,700 Royalists.

The castle stands on a small plateau, above Morpeth and with fine views of it, but completely removed from the bustle. Once inside the curtain wall, whose circuit is battered but still complete, you could be inside the most remote Border stronghold.

Attic floor

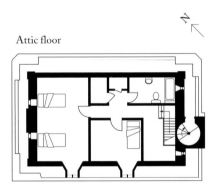

Second floor

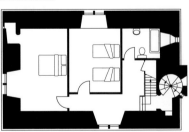

First floor

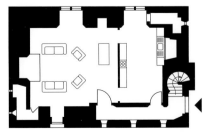

# The Music Room

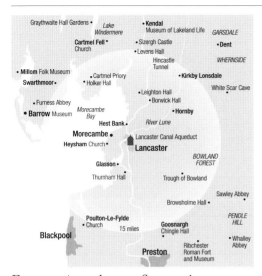

For up to 4 people
Roof terrace

Steep staircase
Parking for 1 car

The Music Room had been well known for years as a building in distress, but nothing could be done because it had other buildings hard up against it on all four sides. On our first visit we had to reach it by walking through the toy warehouse of which it formed a part. We had to buy all these buildings and demolish them (a long job) to give the builders access.

It seems to have been built in about 1730 as a garden pavilion, but its surroundings have long been overlaid with streets. In the nineteenth century it became part of a stained-glass factory. When we arrived it had a temporary roof and many broken windows. Most of the plasterwork had fallen, but luckily almost all of it was in the building.

We turned the loggia into a shop by glazing the central Ionic arch and removing an inserted floor; it did not seem sensible to leave this large space lifeless and empty in the middle of a town. In front, with the City's help, we made a pedestrian square.

The plasterwork of the music room itself took 6,000 hours of work to repair. It is an exceptional Baroque interior. On the walls are the muses: eloquence, history, music, astronomy, tragedy, rhetoric, dancing, comedy and amorous poetry; with Apollo over the fireplace. A fruitful goddess with a torch presides over the ceiling. One muse had vanished entirely and was recreated by the plasterers from Sutton Coldfield as a modern girl, big and busty, with a cheerful eye; she makes an excellent muse of dancing.

In the attic above, reached by a narrow stair, we made a flat. From it and from the small terrace on its roof there are distant views over Lancaster (including a fine view of the Castle from the sink); and at all times, waiting for you to enter it, there is the stillness of the music room below, both full and empty at the same time, as is the way with rich interiors. Lancaster is a fine town, with many things worthy of attention, not least Rennie's monumental aqueduct on the Lancaster Canal, bridging the River Lune like a vestige of imperial Rome.

Second floor

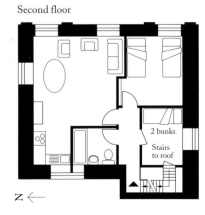

The bunks are narrow, more suitable perhaps for children than adults.

# New Inn

Peasenhall, Suffolk

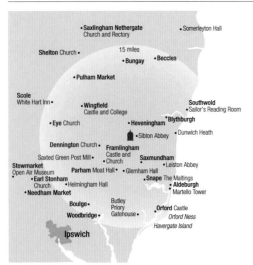

**High End**
For up to 4 people
Shared garden
Adjacent parking

**Low End**
For up to 4 people
Open fire
Shared garden
Adjacent parking

**The Cottage**
For up to 5 people
Shared garden
Parking nearby
Steep staircase
Low ceiling on
upper floors

All have shared
use of the hall

The centre of this handsome range of buildings is a late medieval hall-house, in use as an inn by 1478, and almost certainly built as such. Inns were then a fairly new invention, which had arrived in response to an increase in trade and therefore of travellers. It was some time before they evolved into a distinct building type, however; until then most kept to the basic form that everyone knew, of a hall with chambers off it – and this is just what there is at the New Inn.

We repaired the hall and all the other cottages in the row as well. The three oldest we kept as Landmarks. Two of them, at each end of the impressive hall, are entered from it, as they would have been originally. (The hall is open to the public and is sometimes visited.) The high end is the grander, with one particularly fine bedroom – a solar or great chamber with a crown-post roof.

At the backs of the cottages we removed some decayed sheds to make a garden and a place to hide cars. We also bought the land in front, closed the road that ran across it, and turned it into a village green. Peasenhall is a long, open village, with a stream running beside the road. It is much-visited by connoisseurs of sausages and ham, sold in more than one of its excellent shops. Add oysters from Orford, fish from Aldeburgh, wines from Framlingham vineyards, and sit down to your own feast in the lofty hall, as might those medieval travellers over 500 years ago.

From the logbook
*Spent hours studying the beautiful carpentry of the building's oak frame.*

*The Landmark Trust library here is too good. Too much interest and no time to read.*

Ground floor        First floor        Second floor

High End

Hall

Low End

The Cottage

2 bunks

Upper part of Hall

Attic

Attic

N

# Nicolle Tower

St Clement's, Jersey

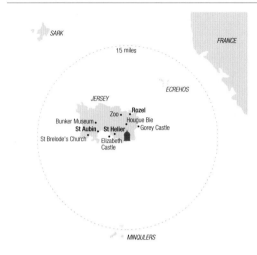

For up to 2 people
Garden

Adjacent parking
Steep staircase

We were reluctant to take on this building until we actually went to see it. As often, there proved to be much more to it, and to the place, than a description or a snapshot could convey. Therefore we bought it, and its owner also sold us the field of five vergees in which the tower stands.

The field is called Le Clos de Hercanty. Hercanty means 'tilted menhir', and one corner of the tower, tantalisingly, is built on a large half-buried slab of diorite. Moreover, on this boulder is carved a compass rose and a date, 1644, so something has been going on here for a long time. It seems that the menhir was once a navigation mark, next to which a small rectangular lookout was built. In 1821 Philippe Nicolle, who had just bought the field, added a light-hearted Gothick octagon with the present very pretty sitting-room on the first floor.

In 1943 the Germans, to make an observation or control position here, astutely raised the roof of the octagon by one more storey, so that no change would be noticed from the air. As this latest addition is part of the history of the tower, we have left it there, with its slit eyes and German ranging marks on its thick concrete ceiling. The tower stands 160 feet up, well back from the coast, with, it need hardly be said, views over the sea and island in every direction.

From the logbook
*Peace, lovely walks, our own tower to live in – what more could you want?*

Ground floor

First floor

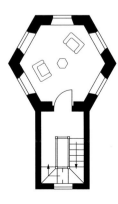

Second floor

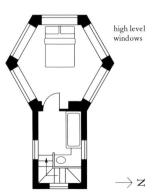

high level windows

→ N

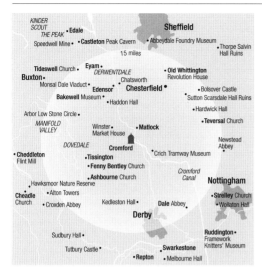

For up to 4 people
Open fire
Enclosed garden

Parking nearby
Steep staircase
Dogs allowed

To stay here is to stay in an important piece of history, because North Street is the earliest planned industrial housing in the world and the finest of its type ever built – vastly superior to that of the next century, and now lying at the heart of a designated World Heritage Site. It was built in 1771 by Richard Arkwright to house his mill workers, and named after the Prime Minister. The three-storey gritstone houses have one room on each floor, with a room for framework-knitting in the attic. Each has a small garden and an allotment at a distance. No. 10 has a croft, or paddock, as well, at the back of the houses, which our visitors (and their children) can use.

We bought six of the houses in 1974 from the Ancient Monuments Society, which had taken them on to save them from demolition. We then bought a further three houses on the same side of the street. We re-roofed and improved all nine, and restored the long windows of the attic workrooms, keeping the original interiors where they survived. One house (No. 10) we repaired as a Landmark so that people can live in and appreciate this much-inhabited street and explore its remarkable surroundings.

All around there is much to enjoy in the Peak District, and, for those interested in industrial history, there is a great deal to see – lead mines, the Cromford canal, the High Peak Railway, Arkwright's mills, and traces of the life they created. There is also Matlock Bath and Matlock, a genuine inland resort, at whose petrifying wells you can have your bowler hat turned into stone.

From the logbook
*The house is better than my wildest dreams; one suggestion – how about a fireman's pole instead of the stairs?*

No. 10 is the second house from the right.

Ground floor

Stairs to garden

First floor

Second floor

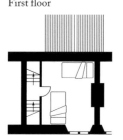

# Obriss Farm

Near Westerham, Kent

For up to 5 people
Open fire

Garden
Adjacent parking

Obriss Farm sits on the lower slopes of Toys Hill, looking South over the Weald. It was given to us by the executors of Mrs Helena Cooper – 160 acres, mainly of pasture, with some woods, and at the centre, well away from any roads, a compact group of buildings which, with their mixture of brick, timber and tile, fit comfortably into the landscape. The field pattern here has not changed since 1840, probably even before that. Besides the farmhouse in which you stay and a smoke house behind it with a tall chimney, all the traditional buildings are here: byres, stable and sheds round the yard in front of the house, and off to one side the great threshing barn. A sheep farmer continues to farm the land around and uses some of the outbuildings for lambing and other purposes. The gentle activity which goes on around you will be part of the pleasure and interest of staying here, yet surrounded by ancient woodland, Obriss is unexpectedly peaceful, an island out of time in this busy part of the country.

From the logbook
*Difficult to believe we are so close to London when the view from the windows convinces us we are alone in Eden.*

*We didn't need to count the sheep to fall asleep.*

*We felt generations of people having lived with us.*

Ground floor

First floor

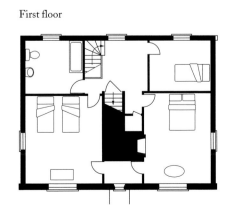

N
↑

# Old Campden House

Chipping Campden, Gloucestershire

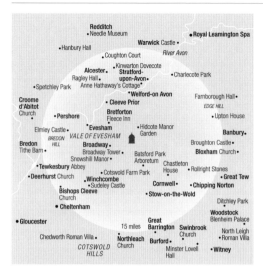

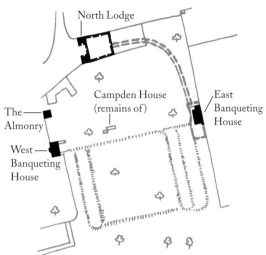

Two banqueting houses, one for 6 and one for 4.

In 1613 the newly enriched Sir Baptist Hicks began work on a house in Chipping Campden. It was a noble work in the latest fashion, with intricate gardens. 30 years later it was destroyed, wantonly, by the Royalists, when in 1645 they withdrew from the town. 'The house (which was so faire) burnt,' noted one, sadly.

Only a shell was left, now shrunk to a single fragment. But other, lesser, buildings escaped the fire, and are still there, together with the raised walks of the garden.

The ogee domes of the lodges are well known, but in the field beyond are two banqueting houses with ebullient strapwork parapets which have been given to us by a descendant of Sir Baptist, together with the lodges, the small building known as the Almonry and the historic site.

The banqueting houses stand at either end of the broad terrace that ran along the garden front of the house. Sir Baptist would bring his guests to them at the end of dinner, to drink rare wines, eat dried fruit and sweetmeats, and admire his domain. After the razing of the main house, the passing years have given each banqueting house its separate history and character, which we have acknowledged adjusting them for use as Landmarks.

To get to either, you must walk along a grassy path, leaving your car just outside in the former henyard. Both banqueting houses have their annexes, the North Lodge or the Almonry. Whether you choose to sip Tokay and nibble the crystallised petals of a flower, or make do with fish and chips and beer, in this place it cannot fail to taste sublime.

*The grounds will be open to the public on certain days during the year but this is most unlikely to happen while the buildings are occupied.*

# Old Campden House

## East Banqueting House

Deceptively diminutive from the terrace, this banqueting house has two further floors below, hidden by the lie of the land, once holding a self-contained apartment and executed with crisp Jacobean élan. It overlooks the Coneygree, an ancient ground now owned by the National Trust and no doubt the scene of many a hare course for the entertainment of Sir Baptist's guests after dinner. More recently, in the nineteenth century, the Earl of Gainsborough used the loggia to review his militia as they ran through their drill on the Coneygree. A further twin bedroom and bathroom are provided in one of the pepperpot lodges – this time as diminutive as it looks.

For up to 6 people
Solid fuel stove
Open grounds
Parking nearby
Steep staircases

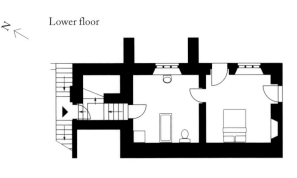

Lower floor

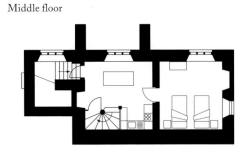

Middle floor

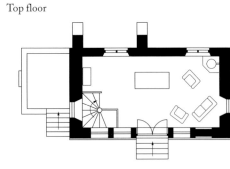

Top floor

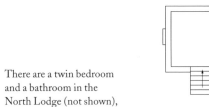

There are a twin bedroom and a bathroom in the North Lodge (not shown), a short walk away.

# West Banqueting House and Almonry

The West Banqueting House is also more spacious than it looks, with a large, barrel vaulted chamber on the ground floor and a hearth at either end – perhaps once a kitchen, as it now is again. The first floor chamber yields the only fragments of Jacobean frieze of the rich and elegant plasterwork and panelling that must once have adorned all the buildings on this site. Yet this banqueting house was converted at an early stage for humbler domestic accommodation and it may well have been the house of William Harrison, steward to Lady Juliana Hicks and a key player in the mystery known as The Campden Wonder. We have allowed this era to continue to speak in the building, by keeping a rough studwork partition and leaving the loggia windows blocked, as we found them. There is a further sitting-room and twin bedroom (with cunningly concealed bathroom) in the little building across the former bleach garden, known as the Almonry for its proximity to Sir Baptist's fine almshouses. It was previously rescued from decay in the 1920s by F. L. Griggs, providing a happy link with the Arts & Crafts movement that continues to flourish in Chipping Campden to this day.

For up to 4 people
Open fire and solid fuel stove
Open grounds
Adjacent parking
Steep and narrow stairs

The West Banqueting House, *above*, *left* and *far left*

The Almonry

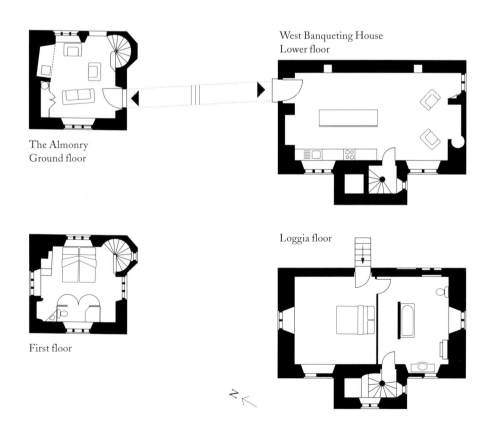

The Almonry
Ground floor

First floor

West Banqueting House
Lower floor

Loggia floor

# The Old Hall

Croscombe, Somerset

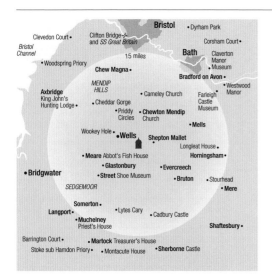

For up to 5 people
Solid fuel stove
Enclosed garden

Parking nearby
Dogs allowed

Originally the great hall of a manor house built by Sir William Palton in about 1420, this building was for 250 years a Baptist chapel. It lies just north of the handsome parish church and looks into a small tranquil enclosure, part garden and part graveyard.

The Baptists, but for whom the building would certainly have disappeared, made a number of harmless alterations. Removal of these – and the repair and consolidation of the tottering structure, with its wavy roof of pantiles, like a shaken rug – revealed quite a grand hall with a particularly fine arch-braced open roof.

In its south wall we found the great blocked arch of an oriel chamber, which once linked the hall to a vanished wing to the east. Beside it a rare medieval light-bracket appeared, decorated with the arms of Sir William and his wife. The service end of the hall we turned into bedrooms and kitchen, simple rooms of wood and stone.

When working on this building, we were offered a fully operational Gurney's Patent Stove from Romsey Abbey, which we installed here to give extra heat in the hall, a challenge in view of its size. Keeping it stoked up provides much entertainment, and some strenuous exercise.

From the logbook
*Though we sought out two other 15th century hall houses we saw nothing as fine as this great hall.*

*Years spent as an archaeologist working on ruins cannot equal the pleasure of living in the real thing.*

N
↑

Ground floor

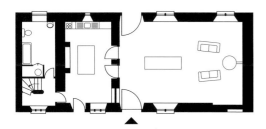

First floor

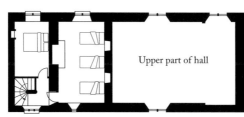

Upper part of hall

# The Old Parsonage

Iffley, Oxford

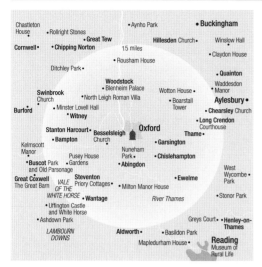

For up to 6 people
Open fire
Garden parking area

Dogs allowed
Riverside garden

Not only an important building in its own right, this house also conveys a strong impression of a parson's life in former days. A rectory was first built here at the same time as the elaborate Norman church a few yards away (and the earlier half of the house still is a rectory, modernised by us). In about 1500, a smart new wing was added, and in it are the handsome rooms that you can occupy. Some of them were later panelled and given new fireplaces. In the parlour, probably added when J. C. Buckler worked on the house in 1857, is a tremendous Latin inscription running round the room. It says, in tall Gothic letters, 'For we know that, if our earthly house were destroyed, we have a building of God, a house not made with hands, eternal in the heavens'. Here, within its dark temporal panels, you may sit looking down the garden, as did many a scholarly leisured parson, pondering his sermon as he watched the Thames slide by.

The staircase, in a square tower of its own, is strong and plain, and reminiscent of staircases in Oxford colleges nearby. The house is entered straight off the pavement of Mill Lane, giving no hint of the long garden on the other side running down to the river at the tail of Iffley lock. The contrast is very agreeable.

From the logbook
*In Oxford we walked in the footsteps of Inspector Morse and enjoyed it thoroughly.*

*Seriously considering never going home…*

Ground floor

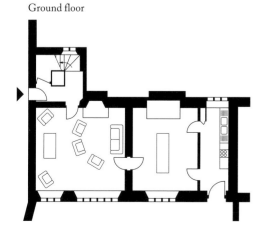

First floor

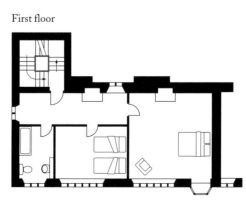

Second floor

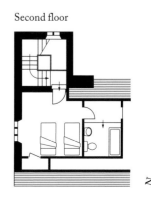

# Old Place of Monreith

Portwilliam, Dumfries and Galloway

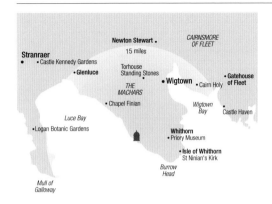

For up to 8 people
Solid fuel stove and open fire
Enclosed garden

Adjacent parking
Spiral staircase
Dogs allowed

The Old Place, also known as Dowies, is a house that was left behind by the family that built it when they prospered and went to live in a castle they bought nearby in 1683. It then became a farmhouse on their estate.

Before that, however, it was the home of the Maxwells, forebears of both Sir Herbert, historian and gardener, and the author Gavin Maxwell and his brother, Sir Aymer Maxwell, who arranged its transfer to us. Built in about 1600, it is a typical, plain, lowland laird's house, still nominally fortified, at the end of a long uneven track.

When we bought it, it had been empty for 20 years. The roof and floors had fallen in, but two good fireplaces survived inside. We opened up the turnpike stair, which had been bricked up, and unblocked the main door with its stone panel for a coat of arms above.

The sea is only two miles away – the same coastline on which the Maxwell brothers grew up, at Elrig, seven miles away. Whithorn, across the peninsula, was a centre of early Christian culture around the Irish Sea, which produced such saints as Ninian, Patrick and Columba. A cross once stood near the Old Place but was moved in the nineteenth century and is now in Whithorn museum. There remains behind a strong sense of a continuous civilised life, lived here over two millennia, in a place that, even for a Landmark, is exceptionally quiet and remote.

From the logbook
*The walk to St Ninian's cave was beautiful – full of bluebells.*

*Powerful sense of an ancient culture and sense of peace which has cast a spell on us all.*

*Wigtown, the Scottish book town, now has 23 bookshops.*

*Sunset over the Torhousie stone circle!*

Ground floor

First floor

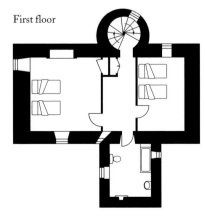

Attic floor

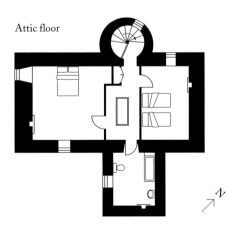

# Parish House

Baltonsborough, Somerset

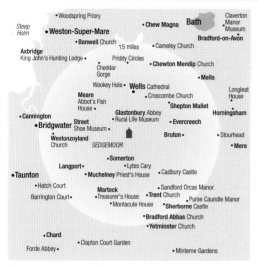

For up to 4 people
Solid fuel stove
Garden

Parking nearby
Dogs allowed

This is a rare example of a church house that has remained in the ownership and use of the parish. We have been brought in to preserve the link but to take on its care. Built in about 1500, on the edge of the churchyard, it has long served the village of Baltonsborough for meetings and festivals, both formal and convivial.

We have improved the parish meeting room on the ground floor, which still has its great hearth across one end. Above, in the part you can stay in, was a long room with an open arch-braced roof. The Tudor churchwardens exercised great economy in their building works: no timber is heavier than it need be. When this floor was later fitted out for a tenant, similar frugality ensured that the alterations were minimal and undamaging.

The long room was divided by an oak partition, which we have kept, but the graceful arched trusses still rise over your head on each side of it. From the windows of the main rooms there is a fine view of the church itself. This is entirely fifteenth century and is dedicated to St Dunstan, Abbot of Glastonbury and Archbishop of Canterbury in the reign of Edgar the Peaceable. Under Dunstan's patronage, art and learning flourished, and after his death he was chosen as England's first patron saint.

From the logbook
*Blissful, enchanting and deeply peaceful. Will never forget lying in that great bed on a sunlit morning with blossom and church song blowing in through the window.*

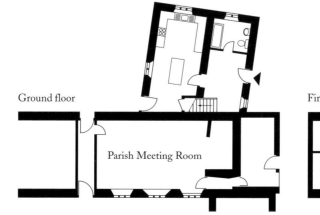

Ground floor

Parish Meeting Room

N

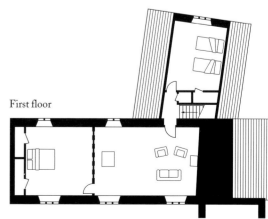

First floor

# Paxton's Tower Lodge

Llanarthney, Camarthenshire

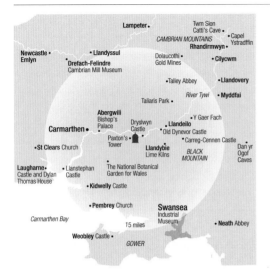

For up to 5 people
Open fire
Enclosed garden

Parking nearby
Dogs allowed

We acquired this building as part of a joint scheme with the National Trust to preserve Paxton's Tower and its surroundings. It is an early nineteenth-century cottage of well above average quality, built for the tower's caretaker, looking south over an immense expanse of country. It is difficult to imagine a finer view. If, however, you walk a hundred yards or so up the small green hill behind, to the foot of the Tower, there, in the opposite direction, is the finer view – surely one of the best in Britain, a prospect extensive and rich, embracing the whole vale of the Tywi, whose green windings your eye can follow for 30 miles or more.

Paxton's Tower itself, which attracts its share of summertime visitors, was built in about 1811, to designs by S. P. Cockerell, ostensibly as a memorial to Nelson but also as an eye-catcher for Middleton Hall, long since demolished but whose footprint is now preserved at the heart of the National Botanic Gardens of Wales. Our cottage has an interesting arrangement inside, partly due to remodelling by us, and a handsome, very low-beamed attic.

From the logbook
*On Wednesday morning nine deer were in the wood next to the cottage.*

*… the farmer rounding up his sheep on stout mountain pony with aid of whistle and those highly intelligent dogs, fascinating to watch.*

*We love the way the dome of the National Botanic Garden keeps a steady eye on Paxton's Tower.*

Ground floor

First floor

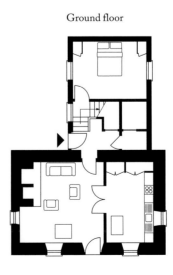

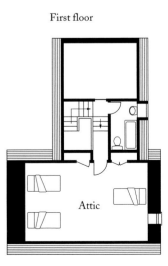

Attic

The attic bedroom has very low beams.

# Peake's House

Peake's House stands in the Dutch Quarter, north of the High Street, which has retained its old street plan and many of its old houses. Here Flemish weavers settled in the 1570s, driven into exile by religious persecution. Colchester had astutely applied to the Privy Council for permission to receive a colony. Trade revived as a result and Colchester baize became a lucrative export for over a century.

Colchester deals in superlatives – the oldest recorded town, the earliest Roman colony, the largest Norman castle, the finest oysters. It offers much else besides, a thriving market town (on some evenings, even a little too lively) with a long and visible history, on the southern edge of East Anglia.

The building has been leased to us by the Borough Council, to which it was given in 1946, by Mr W. O. Peake, who owned a factory and much other property nearby. For many years let to the Red Cross, the house was in need of a new use, which we now provide.

From the logbook
*Marvellous creaky old galleon of a house.*

*Such a snug house.*

*Great to leave the car in one place and for everything to be on the doorstep.*

For up to 4 people
Open fire
Enclosed garden

Adjacent parking for 1 car
Steep staircase

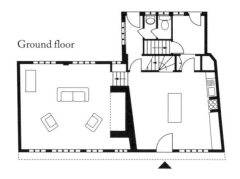

Ground floor

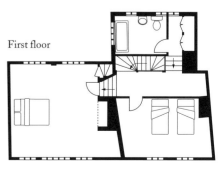

First floor

# Peppercombe

Horns Cross, North Devon

Two houses for up to 3 and 4 people.

The cliffs of the North Devon coast around Bideford Bay are broken by deep valleys that run almost down to the sea, but not quite. At the mouth there is usually a drop of some feet to the shore, down which tumbles a stream. Peppercombe is just such a valley, steep and wooded, and then opening out into a meadow, suspended 40 feet or more above the beach. The stream goes straight down the final stretch in a fine waterfall, but there is no need for you to do the same, thanks to a gently sloping path. The cliffs themselves are particularly dramatic here, formed from an outcrop of red Triassic stone. The whole magnificent coastline curves away in both directions, with Lundy on the horizon.

For centuries the combe belonged to the Portledge estate, and the Coffin family (latterly Pine-Coffins). In 1988 it was acquired by the National Trust, and we took on two of the buildings.

From the logbook
*Landmarks are not simply places to stay, but places in which it is a pleasure to stay.*

## Bridge Cottage

Bridge Cottage, built in about 1830, stands in woods at the top of the combe. It had been empty for years, with a tarpaulin over its roof, but the walls of cob and stone were sound. The kitchen and parlour have stone-flagged floors and fireplaces, while the bedrooms follow the line of the roof and seem slightly too small for furniture, as cottage bedrooms should.

For up to 3 people
Open fire
Sloping garden
Parking nearby
Uneven sloping approach path
Dogs allowed

Ground floor

First floor

# Castle Bungalow

At the mouth of the combe is Castle Bungalow, which is just that, a 1920s Boulton and Paul bungalow. The company's archivist (it is still going strong in Norwich) found one catalogue of this period for us; it had survived the bombing of the factory in 1940. It has tempting illustrations of 'Residences, Bungalows and Cottages', ranging from a substantial six-bedroom house on two storeys (at £4,000) to Bungalow B49, with just a bedroom, a living-room and a verandah (in case you should live in the tropics). This, with brick foundations and carriage paid to the nearest goods station, cost just £280.

Sadly, although a number of its brothers and sisters are there, our bungalow does not feature in the catalogue, but it is still just as tempting. Its weather-boarded walls are painted in railway colours, cream and brown (like the old Great Western Railway carriages), its windows are latticed, and inside the rooms are snug as only wood-lined rooms can be. Beside it are the remains of Peppercombe Castle, a castellated seaside residence.

For up to 4 people
Solid fuel stove
Wild meadow garden
Adjacent parking
Dogs allowed

From the logbook
*Our little girl (three and a half) loved this place and thought she was staying in the wooden house that belonged to one of the three pigs.*

2 bunks

N

# Peters Tower

Lympstone, Devon

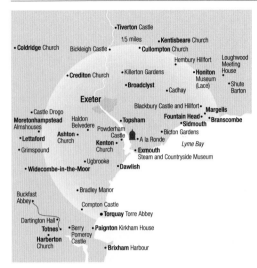

For up to 2 people
No private parking

Steep spiral staircase

The Peters family were successful Liverpool merchants who, in the nineteenth century, served their country as soldiers, sailors and landowners. William Peters, who built this clock tower in 1885 as a memorial to his wife Mary Jane, was in the 7th Dragoons and lived in a sizable classical house nearby. His son was a General and his grandson an Admiral. On the latter's death in 1979 the Trustees of his estate offered us the tower as a gift.

It is no great work of architecture – a very distant and poor relation of St Mark's in Venice – but it is part of the history of Lympstone, and it does stand, at the end of an alley, actually on the water's edge in this large and pleasant village, looking across the broad estuary of the Exe to the green fields beyond. Moreover, it is only a short walk from a railway station, so there is no need for those who stay here to have a car.

Accordingly we took it on, repaired the polychrome brick, restored the clock, and made the tower habitable again – it had been a refuge for fishermen stranded here by the weather. Every inch of space inside its tiny rooms is valuable, so our architect, having spent some time at a boatyard, fitted it out with teak and brass and varnish. The views from all the windows are interesting and some spectacular, and there is a good deal of boating and sailing to be watched or participated in.

From the logbook
*Three pubs, a restaurant, and a station within two minutes' walk.*

*The sanctuary of the Tower seemed like a sleek racing yacht turned through 90 degrees and planted by its stem in the beach.*

Third floor

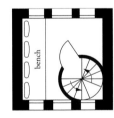

2 bunks

Second floor

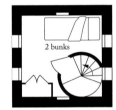

bench

First floor

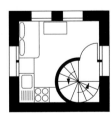

Ground floor

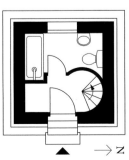

# The Pigsty

Robin Hood's Bay, North Yorkshire

For up to 2 people
Enclosed sloping
garden

Parking nearby
Steep steps from
parking place

Two pigs were the excuse for this exercise in primitive classicism, supposedly inspired by buildings seen by Squire Barry of Fyling Hall on his travels around the Mediterranean in the 1880s. By his use of timber columns, and his choice of inhabitants, he was perhaps trying to make a point about the roots of Classical architecture; or it may just have been that, as in the song, 'there was a lady loved a swine'. In Walter Crane's illustration for this song (from *The Baby's Opera*, published in 1877), the sty is given a Classical front, which might have been the starting point for Barry's eclectic inspiration.

The pigs' owners lived in a pair of neighbouring cottages, also architecturally embellished, but this time in more traditional Estate Gothic. It is several decades since they went in for pig-breeding, and alternative uses were hard to think of, until its owner heard of our activities and later gave us a long lease. By the minimum of addition, and the insertion of glass here and there, we hope that we have made it acceptable (if not entirely draught-free) to a higher breed of inhabitant; and although the living quarters will never be palatial, the view over hills and towards Robin Hood's Bay from under the pediment is undoubtedly fit for an Empress.

From the logbook
*This is only our 7th Landmark but the stays in them represent the 7 best times I've had in my life.*

*Walking in North Yorkshire is endless in possibilities.*

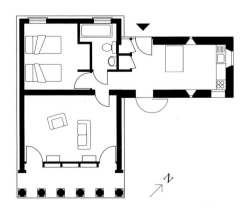

# The Pineapple

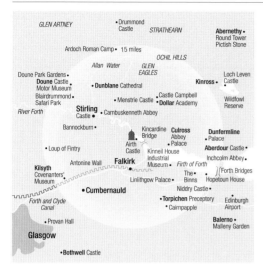

For up to 4 people    Parking nearby
Open fire    Dogs allowed
Garden

The Pineapple is an elaborate summerhouse of two storeys, built for the 4th Earl of Dunmore. Though classical and orthodox at ground level, it grows slowly into something entirely vegetable; conventional architraves put out shoots and end as prickly leaves of stone. It is an eccentric work, of undoubted genius, built of the very finest masonry.

It probably began as a pavilion of one storey, dated 1761, and only grew its fruity dome after 1777, when Lord Dunmore was brought back, forcibly, from serving as Governor of Virginia. There, sailors would put a pineapple on the gatepost to announce their return home. Lord Dunmore, who was fond of a joke, announced his return more prominently.

The Pineapple presides over an immense walled garden. This, in the Scottish tradition, was built some distance from the house, to take advantage of a south-facing slope. To house the gardeners, stone bothies were built on either side of the Pineapple. These make plain, unassuming rooms to stay in, though you have to go out of doors to get from one part to the other.

The Pineapple and its surroundings are owned by the National Trust for Scotland; we took a long lease in 1973 and restored all the buildings and the walled garden, which is now open to the public. At the back, where the ground level is higher, is a private garden for our visitors, with steps leading into the elegant room inside the Pineapple itself.

From the logbook
*The experience of actually living in such a building is so much more rewarding than merely visiting.*

*Hooray for the Pineapple, prickly and proud.*

*Farewell, old fruit.*

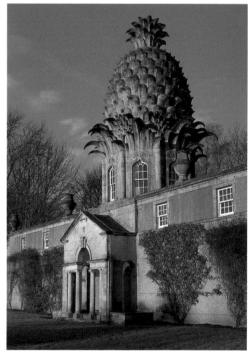

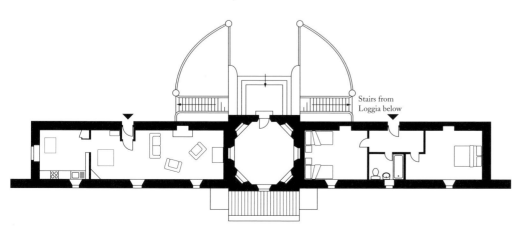

Stairs from
Loggia below

N

# Plas Uchaf

Near Corwen, Powys

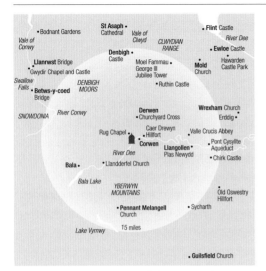

For up to 4 people
Open fire
Garden

Adjacent parking
Dogs allowed

This substantial hall-house was built in about 1400, or perhaps before, on the side of a low hill in the Dee valley. Few houses of this age and type survive in Wales, and the quality of the work at Plas Uchaf is exceptional.

It was in the last stages of dereliction when we arrived here, but the oak frames of medieval houses are remarkably tough, particularly where they have been smoked for generations by the open hearth. Its repair was still possible, and well worthwhile.

The hall is surprisingly grand, with a spere truss, two other moulded trusses, traces of a louvre, and wind and ridge braces – a roof of sophisticated carpentry. In the sixteenth century an immense fireplace was added, which, to a degree, heats this grand space. The alterations necessary to achieve modern standards of heating seemed too intrusive here, and we guessed that true Landmarkers would agree that extra jumpers were a better answer. The fire and the hall are the twin spirits of Plas Uchaf, and at night, with the wooden ribs of the hall moving a little in the firelight, you can imagine that you are Jonah inside the whale.

From the logbook
*Thank you Plas Uchaf, Landmark, Mrs Jones, the chap for the logs, Mr Evans the singing butcher, our farmer friend up the road who supplied fresh milk and eggs and many a chat, and farmer Tudor.*

*The pubs in Cynwyd are probably open even if they look shut.*

*You can't really appreciate the hall without the smell and light of the fire.*

Ground floor

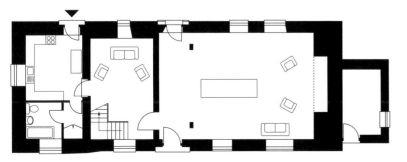

First floor

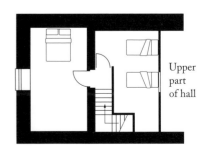

Upper
part
of hall

# Poultry Cottage

Leighton, Welshpool, Powys

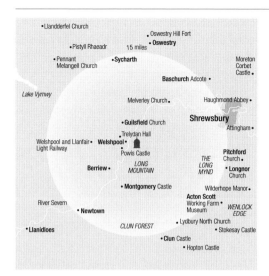

For up to 4 people
Solid fuel stove and
open fire

Garden
Parking nearby
Dogs allowed

Leighton is a model estate on a stupendous scale, laid out in the 1850s by John Naylor, a Liverpool banker with a great deal of money to spend. Besides magnificent housing for all kinds of livestock, the estate had its own aqueduct and cable railway to take water, manure and feed to outlying farms.

The Poultry Yard was added in 1861, complete with fowl house, storm shed, pond and scratching yard, and the poultry-keeper's cottage in which you can stay (but the chickens have long gone). The architect was probably W. H. Gee of Liverpool, who was also responsible for Leighton Hall and Church. The design may have been inspired by Her Majesty's Poultry Houses at Windsor, much praised in Dickson's Poultry of 1853. Each species, whether large or small, ornamental, water or humble hen, had its own meticulously designed quarters: a thorough attention to detail, which is typical of the whole estate.

Another of Mr Naylor's interests was forestry (the Leyland Cypress was first propagated here). Near the Poultry Yard is a grove of giant redwoods, which now belongs to the Royal Forestry Society. Across the Severn Valley are the green hills of Montgomeryshire. There, too, is Powis Castle with its hanging garden, the nearest thing that Wales has to a royal palace.

From the logbook
*This was an ideal refuge from life. The silence is really startling for those of us used to cars, trains and planes.*

*Landmarks never fail to impress. Poultry Cottage is no exception being a magnificent restoration in a remarkable setting.*

*Sweet, very comfortable cottage beautifully presented.*

*It was glorious sitting outside the house watching a glorious sunset.*

Ground floor

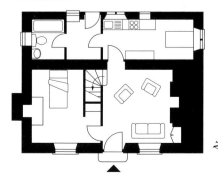

First floor

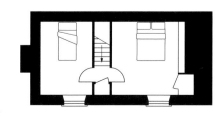

# The Priest's House

Holcombe Rogus, Devon

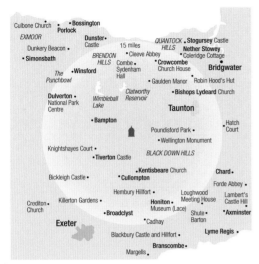

For up to 5 people
Open fire

Parking nearby
Dogs allowed

The Priest's House should really be called the Church House, because that is what it was, acting as half village hall and half inn. Parish feasts were held here on saints' days and other festivals, and hospitality was offered to guests. It had a kitchen and probably a brewery. Many church houses later became pubs, and survive as such to this day.

This one was probably built around 1500; it has fine moulded beams and a cooking hearth across one end, with another fireplace to warm the main room. By some lucky chance it was never converted to another use, but dwindled instead into a parish store. The reason probably lies in its position, squeezed between the garden of Holcombe Court (a fine Tudor house), the stony church lane and the churchyard.

Several old windows survived and inside, where there was evidence to show they had existed, we put back oak partitions and laid a stone floor so that the main rooms have much the same character as they did when used for village gatherings.

Holcombe Rogus is a comfortable village in a beautiful part of Devon, close to the Somerset border, where ancient lanes take you to unexpected but always rewarding places. The church has a good tower, a chiming clock and the memorable pew of the Bluett family who lived at Holcombe Court until the last century.

From the logbook
*The pull of the night sky just outside the door, the gentle swoop of a passing bat or hoot of a nearby owl – bliss.*

*Fascinating house and good country.*

Ground floor

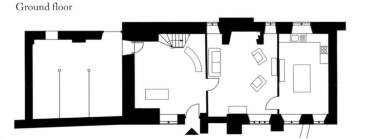

First floor

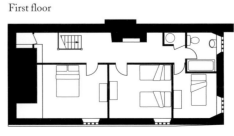

N
↑

# Princelet Street

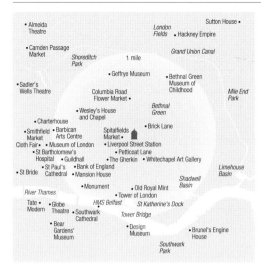

For up to 6 people     Enclosed garden
No private parking

Spitalfields has always been a place where worlds meet. Named after St Marie Spittle, a hospital for the needy founded in the twelfth century, the area sheltered friendly and adventurous foreigners from that time on, living just outside the City walls but originally not admitted to the community of London.

In the late seventeenth and early eighteenth centuries, it was the turn of French Protestants, known as Huguenots, to be washed here by the tide of events, bringing with them their skill and ingenuity. Some were silk weavers, who found an existing incorporation of similar craftsmen already established in Spitalfields. Begun in 1718, Princelet Street contains some of the earliest speculative housing in the area, built to accommodate this new influx.

These are not grand buildings but they are dignified and well-proportioned. They provided their early inhabitants with room both to live and work. (Although this house no longer has its workrooms, others on the street have either attic rooms with the long windows characteristic of the weaver or long,

mansarded outbuildings serving the same purpose.)

The house came to us as a generous bequest from its last owner, Peter Lerwill, who had lovingly restored it. The building retains much of its original floor plan and fabric, most notably its simple panelling, partitions and other joinery.

Today Princelet Street is a quiet street with many of its original buildings. The City of London is but a background hum and yet Liverpool Street Station is only a few minutes walk away. Hawksmoor's Christ Church, built in the same years as Princelet Street and now magnificently restored, stands on the corner, and Norman Foster's 30 St Mary Axe (better known as the Gherkin) is not much farther away. The sleek cliffs of modernist glass along Bishopsgate stand in lieu of the city walls to contrast and complement the more intimate scale of the Spitalfields streets. At the end of Princelet Street is the colour and bustle of Brick Lane. It is an area of festivals and markets, cafes and alleyways, where you will bridge continents and centuries with ease.

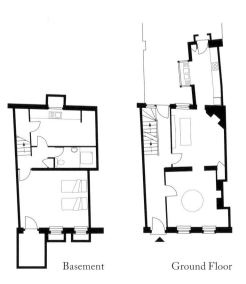

Basement     Ground Floor     First Floor     Second Floor

N

# The Prospect Tower

Belmont Park, Faversham, Kent

For 2 people
Open fire
Garden
Parking nearby

Narrow spiral
staircase
Shower only

This small flint tower stands on the very edge of the garden of Belmont Park (the house was remodelled by Samuel Wyatt in 1792), approached by an avenue of walnut trees. On its other side is a mature park and a now ragged cricket pitch. It was built in about 1808 for General, later Lord, Harris of Seringapatam. He called it his 'Whim', and one suspects that the pleasant upper room, at least, was his own den, into which the family were sometimes allowed for tea.

The General bought Belmont, which owed its name to its 'high situation and extensive prospect', in 1801, with prize money won in India. Farming and gardening were his chief enthusiasms and he soon doubled the size of the pleasure grounds to include the land in which the tower still stands.

The enthusiasm of the 4th Lord Harris was of a different kind. He was one of the fathers of cricket, and it was he who created a pitch in about 1870 and commandeered this tower as a changing room: hooks for the gear still decorate the walls. There are only two rooms in the tower for living and sleeping, but the prospect from its windows is still extensive; and you can dream of all those centuries, hoped for and, sometimes, achieved.

From the logbook
*The best 'prospect' is from the kitchen window.*

*On Sunday morning a balloon went over about 8am – quite unusual to say good morning to its occupants from the top of the tower. They landed on the old cricket pitch.*

*I liked looking down the beautifully kept avenue.*

Ground floor

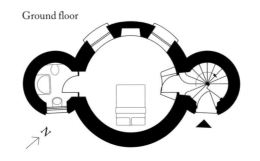

First floor

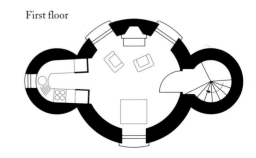

# Purton Green

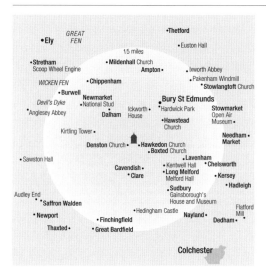

For up to 4 people
Access by footpath
Open grounds

Parking 400 yards
away
Dogs allowed

Purton Green is one of the many lost villages of Suffolk, where generations spent their lives, but which are now just patches of lime and fragments in the plough. It lies on an old road running south from Bury St Edmunds, today hardly a path. All that remains is this house. Inside its late medieval walls survives a hall of 1250 – a great rarity. Aisled on both sides, with scissor-braced trusses and a highly ornamental arcade at the low end, it must once have been an important place.

When we bought it in 1969 it was little more than a ruin. As with almost all medieval houses, a floor and central chimney stack had later been inserted, but these additions were so derelict that we felt justified in removing them, to return the hall to its original open state. Part of the house – the high end – was rebuilt in about 1600 and this part we have turned into living quarters.

These can only be reached through the hall, which you must cross and recross if you stay here, as your predecessors have done for 700 years. The house now stands surrounded by fields, with unchanging Suffolk countryside in all directions. After crossing a ford, you leave your car 400 yards from the house; but we provide a wheelbarrow for the rest of the journey.

From the logbook
*Purton Green provided a fine time machine back to the 13th century for Landmarkers.*

*We spent most of our time there admiring the skill displayed by those who created this enduring structure.*

Ground floor

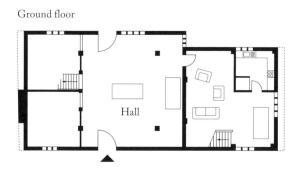

First floor

z ←

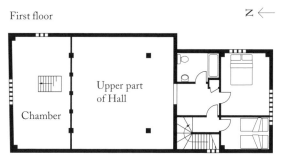

The staircase to the Chamber in the empty part of the building is unenclosed.

# Rhiwddolion

Near Betws-y-coed, Gwynedd

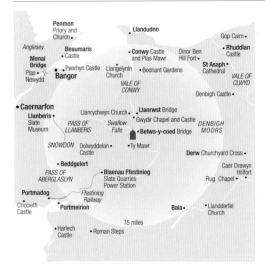

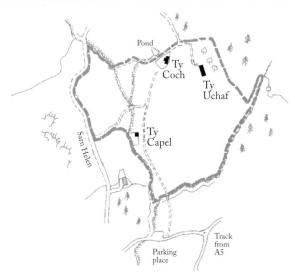

Houses for up to 3, 4 and 2 people.

Rhiwddolion (pronounced Rutholeon) is a remote upland at the head of a valley above Betws-y-coed. For a time there was a slate quarry and community here. Long before that Rhiwddolion was on the Roman road that runs from Merioneth to the Conway valley. It was called Sarn Helen after the mother of the Emperor Constantine, whose father campaigned and died in Britain; Edward I, mindful of this, built Caernarvon Castle with bands of coloured stone, in imitation of Constantinople.

Now, however, Rhiwddolion, with only three houses left besides ours, is given over to the sheep. It is somewhat hemmed in by forestry, but where it remains open, the small-scale landscape of oak trees and rocks emerging from close-cropped pasture is second to none. It is also tranquil and silent except for the sheep and the water; and there is a view far down the valley towards Betws.

It is not possible to get a car to any of our houses; instead, leaving your car by the forestry track, you can walk up (ten minutes, some say longer) on a path of enormous half-buried flagstones, as your predecessors did.

Ty Uchaf

# Ty Capel

Ty Capel, beside the stream that flows down the valley, was a school-cum-chapel in the days of the slate quarry. At the end of the nineteenth century the chapel served a community of 150 people.

Essentially a large single space, with a steep staircase up to the sleeping gallery, this robust stone building is lined with varnished pine, which, to an extent, helps to combat winter cold.

For up to 3 people
Open fire
Access by footpath only
Open grounds
Parking 400 yards away
Dogs allowed

From the logbook
*We came to Ty Capel with the idea of using it as a base to explore North Wales. It exercised its magic on us too, and North Wales went unexplored.*

*Our children speculated for hours on the lives of the children of Rhiwddolion. We took a great delight in the mosses… a perfect place to get to know and understand your family.*

*To my surprise I discovered that I actually quite enjoyed walking.*

*The pair of elderly ladies in the Oxfam shop, Portmadog, sang for us the Welsh hymn written by the schoolmaster of Rhiwddolion.*

Ground floor

First floor
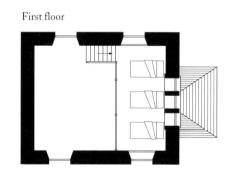

# Rhiwddolion

## Ty Coch

Ty Coch, which means red house, is a few hundred yards higher up from Ty Capel, looking across the head of the valley, by a small waterfall. In origin much older than Ty Capel, it has a stone-flagged living-room with a large open fireplace. The beam that spans this fireplace is a cruck, re-used no doubt from an earlier house that stood here.

For up to 4 people
Solid fuel stove
Access by footpath only
Open grounds
Parking 600 yards away
Dogs allowed

From the logbook
*Idyllic setting, have not seen the like. Children wonderfully content to be around the waterfall and stream.*

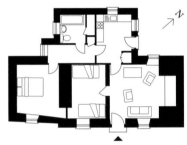

## Ty Uchaf

Ty Uchaf stands at the head of the valley, in the lee of woods rich in mosses and lichens, and looking across the sheep pastures. A datestone for 1685 was found in the tumbledown pigsty. We have respected the original division between the barn and domestic end, and kept part of the crog loft to make a bedroom beneath it. The living-room is open to the roof timbers with a large fireplace under its original bressumer. The tie beam had been cruelly cut some time earlier; we did not repair it, thus keeping an airy space for two. Timbers and walls are all limewashed to enhance the sense of light and space in this modest dwelling. The barn is once again utilitarian, a separate entrance leads into a lobby large enough for all the walking gear you will bring to explore this remote and peaceful place.

For up to 2 people
Open fire
Access by footpath only
Open grounds
Parking 800 yards away
Dogs allowed

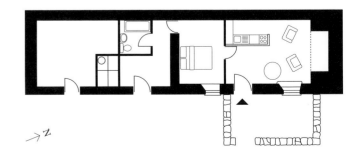

# Robin Hood's Hut

Halswell, Goathurst, Somerset

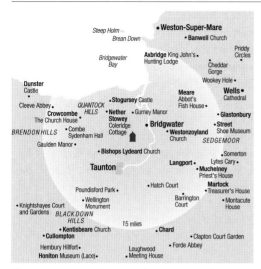

For up to 2 people
Open fire

Adjacent parking
Dogs allowed

It is sometimes surprising to find how far Robin Hood strayed from Sherwood Forest. In fact, the name of this beautiful little pavilion has less to do with our eponymous hero than with Whiggish ideas of liberty and medieval romance in the eighteenth century. In the 1740s Charles Kemeys Tynte began to transform the landscape around Halswell House into one of the finest Georgian gardens in the south west of England. He built several follies within it; by 1767 he was writing to his steward about 'the Building on the Hill of the Park,' instructing that 'the first room, which I call the hermit's room, must have an earthen floor.'

By the time the Somerset Building Preservation Trust came upon Robin Hood's Hut in 1997, it had no roof or windows and had lost much of its plasterwork. Its umbrello was almost gone. After an exemplary restoration of the exterior, the Trust asked Landmark if we would provide a secure future use for the building. We were delighted to help.

Much like The Ruin at Hackfall (page 147), Robin Hood's Hut has two distinct faces and commands a breathtaking panorama.

Approaching through a dark wood, you come upon an apparently rustic cottage, with thatched roof and bark-clad door. Once inside, the elegant interior provides a fitting antechamber to the umbrello, from where the view encompasses the Somerset Levels and Mendip Hills and on across the Bristol Channel to the mountains of South Wales. Like earlier visitors, you too may choose to dine *al fresco* beneath this elegant canopy, whose graceful ogee detailing has more than a hint of the early days of the Raj.

In order not to compromise the views and elegance of a building not designed to hold modern services, we decided to build an equally carefully designed hut of our own to house the bathroom, thus indulging both epochs' notions of civilised existence. Would Robin Hood have approved? We feel sure our present day hermits will, perched above one of the finest views in southern England.

From the logbook
*We've made the most of the umbrello, eating nearly all of our meals out there, and looking out over the views.*

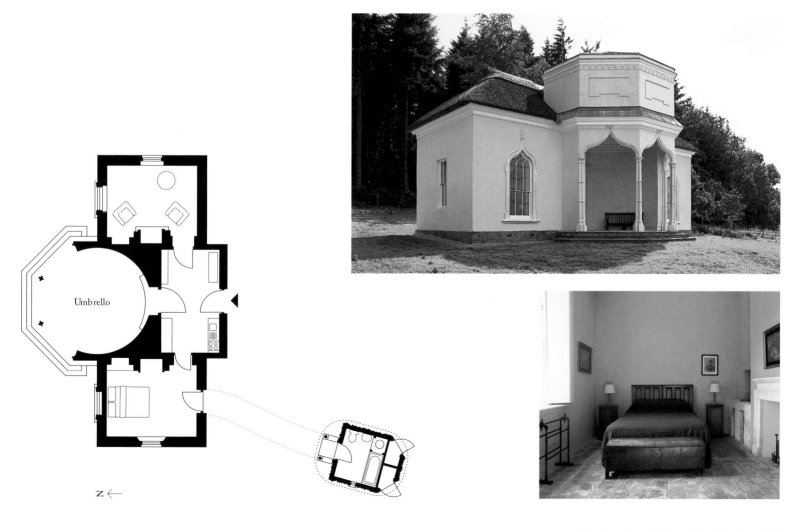

# Roslin

Near Edinburgh

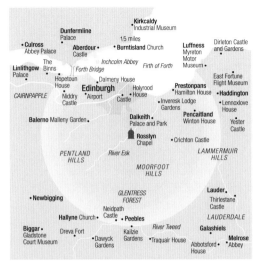

A castle for 7 and a former inn for 6.

The St. Clairs, an ancient Scottish family, have held the Rosslyn estate at Roslin since the early fourteenth century. Rosslyn has long been famous for its picturesque valley, enhanced by generations of St. Clairs with two extraordinary buildings – its ancient castle and a breathtakingly beautiful chapel. The chapel, just outside the village of Roslin, represents the pinnacle of the fifteenth century stonemason's craft, embellished on every surface with sinuous and intricate carving, full of imagery that made the chapel a place of mysticism and pilgrimage even through centuries of dereliction. More recently the present Earl and Countess of Rosslyn have been instrumental in the restoration of both castle and chapel, as well as the house of the former curator to the chapel (which is now happily back in use). To support the Earl in his effort to keep this ancient family's inheritance together, we let both castle and house on his behalf. You can stay in the castle itself or, half a mile away look over the garden wall at the chapel from Collegehill House. As Sir Walter Scott once wrote, 'A morning of leisure can scarcely be anywhere more delightfully spent than in the woods of Rosslyn'.

From the logbook
*… a marvellous base for the Edinburgh Festival.*

*A wild and spectacular setting – it's easy to see why Turner wanted to paint it.*

Rosslyn Castle

# Collegehill House

Many famous travellers have found rest at Collegehill House, former inn and de facto gatehouse to Rosslyn Chapel, a Renaissance jewel lying just over the garden wall. Boswell and Dr. Johnson, Robbie Burns and Francis Grose, J.M.W. Turner and the Wordsworths – even Queen Victoria found hospitality here. Ben Jonson visited the chapel on foot in 1618, to find William Drummond of Hawthornden resting under a tree: 'Welcome, welcome, ye royal Ben', said Drummond, to which Jonson replied with quicker wit than style, 'Thank ye, thank ye, Hawthornden.'

Built in the eighteenth century, Collegehill is not a grand building, but the spot is no less worth seeking out today, the spectacular scenery of the River Esk also lying close by. On the first floor is a grand drawing room with views of the chapel. In the nineteenth century, Roslin became a popular destination for amateur lady painters on day trips from Edinburgh and in this lovely room it is easy enough to conjure up all these many and varied visitors to Roslin as you loll in your armchair with one of the finest expositions of the mason's craft framed in your window.

For up to 6 people
Open fire
Enclosed garden
Adjacent parking
Dogs allowed

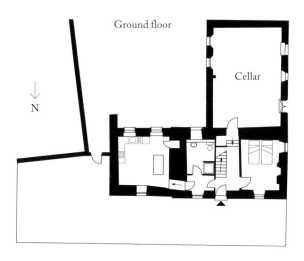

Ground floor

Cellar

N

First floor

# Roslin

## Rosslyn Castle

Most of the castle was built around 1450 by the great William, Prince of Orkney, who lived at Rosslyn in regal state, dining off gold and silver. It was he who built the extraordinary ornament-encrusted chapel of St Matthew at Roslin, one of the wonders of Scotland.

The older fortifications survive only as ruins, but shortly before 1600 Sir William Sinclair replaced the east curtain wall with a more comfortable dwelling, but one which still contains an element of drama. On one side a modest two storey building, on the other it drops five storeys down the side of the rock to reach the ground 60 feet below. Decorated with panelling and moulded plaster ceilings, but later left empty for long periods, the habitable rooms have been restored and furnished by the present Earl of Rosslyn.

For up to 7 people
Solid fuel stove and open fire
Garden
Adjacent parking
Dogs allowed

First floor

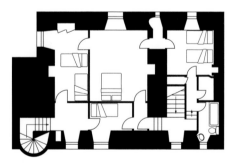

N

Ground floor

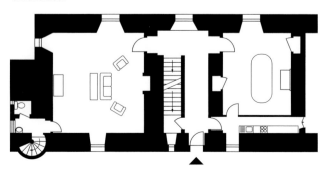

# The Ruin

Hackfall, Grewelthorpe, North Yorkshire

For up to 2 people
Solid fuel stove

Small garden
Parking nearby

However well we get to know our buildings, they can still surprise us. It took Landmark some 15 years to acquire this little pavilion, dramatically perched above a steep wooded gorge in the remnants of an outstanding mid-eighteenth century picturesque garden at Hackfall. The garden was conceived and created by the Aislabies, who also made the gardens at nearby Studley Royal. Hackfall was Studley's antithesis: a 'natural' Gothic landscape with follies, waterfalls and built structures. The Ruin is one of these, a tiny banqueting house which we have allowed to keep its eighteenth-century name, trusting our visitors to share the Aislabies' sense of irony.

The Ruin is a typically Janus-faced Georgian folly: smoothly Gothic on its public elevation, which leads through to a rugged, Romanesque, triple-domed 'ruin' redolent of ancient Rome and Piranesi, and framing a terrace set before one of the finest views in North Yorkshire. It had indeed become a ruin when we set our stonemasons to work to sift, stitch and point it back together. Work was well underway when we had our surprise – a discovery that was, in fact, entirely consistent with Hackfall's pedigree. Our building archaeologist noticed a striking similarity between The Ruin's Romanesque elevation and a watercolour, *Capriccio on Ruins,* by Robert Adam. It offers an unusual example of the work of this greatest of eighteenth-century British architects, better known for his more formally Classical houses and interiors.

The three rooms enclosed by this unique exterior never communicated with each other, and we have kept them so. A richly decorated sitting room is flanked by a bedroom and bathroom; flitting between the two wings across a moonlit terrace is a truly Gothic experience.

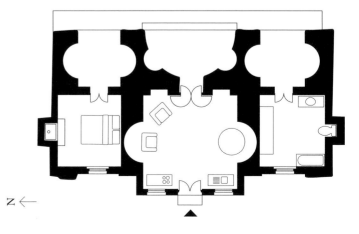

N ←

# Sackville House

East Grinstead, West Sussex

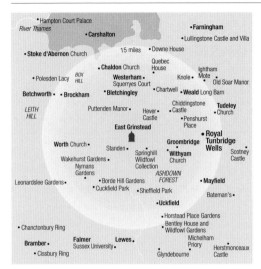

For up to 8 people
Open fire
Enclosed garden

Parking for 3 cars
Dogs allowed

Sackville House was rescued from decay in 1919 by Geoffrey Webb, a stained-glass artist and nephew of Sir Aston Webb, the architect. His daughter left it to us, with the wish that it be kept as a dwelling.

It stands on the south side of East Grinstead's broad High Street. Timber-framed, like most of the older houses here, and roofed in thick Horsham stone, it was built in about 1520 as a hall with chambers at one end, but remodelled 50 years later to form a substantial house running back from the street with a yard at the side.

What is really exceptional about Sackville House lies beyond. East Grinstead was laid out in the thirteenth century, a street of houses each with a long plot of land behind, called a portland. Most of these have since been divided and built on. Only in one small area, opposite the church, do they survive in anything like their original form. The garden here, some 630 feet long, slopes to the South, passing through several stages from formal terrace to wild nuttery. On leaving the High Street and entering the yard, you find yourself with a view of several miles across a wide valley to Ashdown Forest. The contrast, and combination, are delightful.

### From the logbook
*A bustling town with nice shops and restaurants and all the essentials outside the front door, and the countryside in the form of the fantastic garden out of the back door.*

*What a wonderful house; we never tired of looking around.*

Ground floor

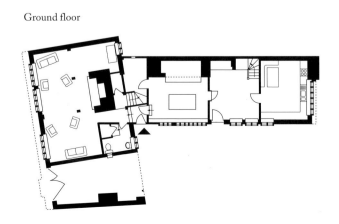

First floor

There is another bathroom in the attic

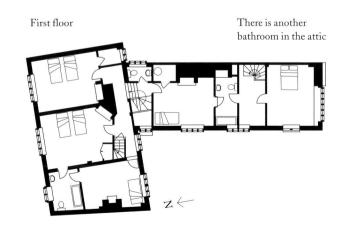

# Saddell

Kintyre, Argyll and Bute

A castle for 8, two houses for 4, one for 5, one for 6 and one for 13.

The fortunate qualities of Saddell have long been recognised. There was an abbey here, sited safely inland. Later it was chosen by the Bishop of Argyll for a new castle, which stands boldly near the shore, by the mouth of a small river looking across to Arran. This castle we now own, together with five houses, the steep old beechwood behind and the whole of Saddell Bay, with its long white strand and rocky point. Those who stay here have the freedom of it all.

Here and there are moulded or carved stones from the ruins of Saddell Abbey, half a mile up the valley. Under the trees in that peaceful place lie many grave slabs of the unruly Scots, gripping their long swords or standing in their ships of war, waiting impatiently for the last trumpet.

From the logbook
*Hire the pipers from Kintyre Motors, Campbeltown, to add to the authenticity of a Scottish evening's reeling on the front lawn.*

*The sea otter is here (if very elusive!) – try the rocks beyond Cul na Shee. Have also spotted heron, kingfisher, swans, adders & basking sharks in the bay.*

*You will always see seals in TorrisdaleBay 10 minutes away.*

Port na Gael is a stone house, which can be used for picnics by those staying at Saddell.

# Saddell

## Cul na Shee

Cul na Shee (or Cul na Sythe) means 'nook of peace' in Gaelic, which in this case refers to a minute bay, backed by steep woods, a few hundred yards beyond the castle. Here in the 1920s a schoolteacher, the daughter of a local minister, built herself a simple home for her retirement, on the grass behind a rocky beach. It would be hard to find a more tranquil place, reached by a path along the beach, overlooked by no other building and with just the sea and Arran to look at. It has, moreover, been a pleasure to preserve a building of a kind so very unfashionable now, to show how suitable it can look and how snug and cheerful its pine-boarded rooms can be.

For up to 4 people
Open fire
Open grounds
Parking a short walk away
Dogs allowed

→ N

## Ferryman's Cottage

Ferryman's Cottage has the same uninterrupted view as Cul na Shee. It was built in about 1930 on the site of a humbler predecessor, the freehold property of an important local figure, the ferryman. Owner of a boat and a house, it was his job to offload provisions from the coastal steamer, or puffer. Before the building of good roads much of Western Scotland was dependent on such deliveries, and Glensaddell was no exception. The house, with light-filled rooms, stands in its own garden, with the remains of the jetty in the rocky bay in front.

For up to 5 people
Open fire
Garden
Adjacent parking
Dogs allowed

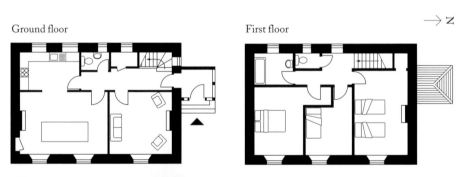

Ground floor

First floor

→ N

# Saddell Castle

Saddell Castle was described as 'a fayre pyle, and a stronge' when it was built in 1508. By 1600 it was firmly in the hands of the Campbells, who thereafter held it for nearly 400 years. It is a fine and complete tower house with a battlemented wall-walk round the roof. When we took it on, there were substantial trees growing from the parapets and all the windows had gone.

Inside, each room is quite different from all the others, and each holds something unexpected and agreeable: panelling or a decorated ceiling, deep window embrasures, or closets in the thickness of the wall. The floor inside the front door is removable so that unwelcome visitors can fall straight into a pit below.

Round a narrow cobbled yard outside, the walls of the attendant outbuildings survive, including part of the old barmkin wall. Built hard up against the castle for protection, they were left because the laird never had any money to spare. Indeed all the later structural repairs seem to have been a struggle, done with whatever lay to hand, even old cart axles.

For up to 8 people
Solid fuel stove
Open grounds
Adjacent parking
Wide spiral staircase
Dogs allowed

First floor

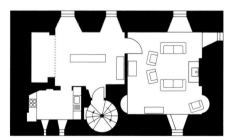

Ground floor

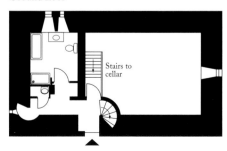

Stairs to cellar

Third floor

Second floor

# Saddell

## Saddell House

Saddell House presides at the centre of the bay, a handsome seat built in 1774 by Colonel Donald Campbell (the Saddell estate had been owned by Campbells since 1600). The Colonel had fought gallantly in India, earning promotion to become Commandant of Madras. He returned to Scotland in 1771, wounded but with rich recompense from the Nawab of Arcot. It was no doubt this that enabled him, even before he entered his inheritance, to build Saddell House, which he positioned on the edge of the beach to take advantage of views across both the Kilbrannan Sound towards Arran and the fertile plain inland. It was a typical Scottish laird's house of its period, with generously proportioned rooms and large light windows.

The house also proved a good base for hunting and fishing and it was while an eventual tenant, a Reverend Bramwell, was out shooting in September 1899 that disaster struck. A chimney fire spread to the attic, destroying the roof and gutting the house. Only the walls and a fine set of service rooms in the basement survived. Fortunately for us, Saddell House was judged worthy of repair and was rebuilt almost at once. It became what it remains today: an eminently sensible Edwardian house for a generation or three to spend a holiday together, close enough to an outdoors life but offering a comfortable haven from the elements when needed. The Morton family lived here until 1998, after which gentle refurbishment was all that was needed to thread this, the last pearl, onto our Saddell string.

For up to 13 people
Open fire
Open grounds
Adjacent parking
Dogs allowed

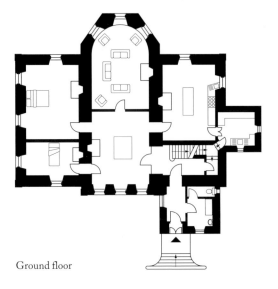

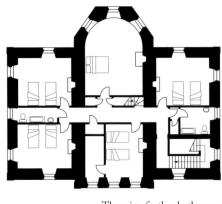

There is a further bathroom on the attic floor.

Ground floor

First floor

N

## Saddell Lodge

Guarding the entrance and wooded drive to the Saddell estate is Saddell Lodge, a handsome granite gate lodge. We do not know exactly when it was built – perhaps when Colonel McLeod was refurbishing the castle in the 1890s, or after the serious fire at Saddell House in 1899. Either way, the lodge avoided any such ravages itself, a simple but considered building to which we added a bedroom. For many years the home of our Regional Property Manager, the lodge now adds its own architectural character to the Landmarks at Saddell, lying snugly at the edge of the estate just across the road from the ruins of Saddell Abbey.

For up to 4 people
Open fire
Open grounds
Adjacent parking
Dogs allowed

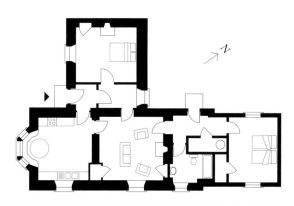

## Shore Cottage

Shore Cottage looks at the castle across a little bay. It stands on a rocky point, among trees that grow right down to the sea, and is a plain but stylish Victorian building, imaginative in design as well as situation. From the sitting room a door leads directly on to the foreshore, where the rock pools at low tide are second to none.

For up to 6 people      Adjacent parking
Solid fuel stove        Dogs allowed
Open grounds

Ground floor

First floor

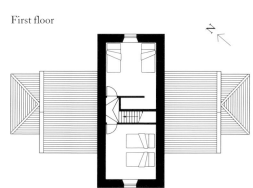

# St Mary's Lane

Tewkesbury, Gloucestershire

**No. 30**
For up to 6 people
Small rear yard
Steep staircase
Parking for 1 car
nearby

**No. 32**
For up to 4 people
Small rear yard
Steep twisting
staircase
No private parking

Two houses, one for 4 and one for 6 people.

In 1969 we came to the rescue of some relics of Tewkesbury's eighteenth century prosperity. 30 and 32 St Mary's Lane are rare survivals of houses designed for framework knitters or stocking makers. An organised but domestic trade, it provided the chief employment of the town for over a century. These tall and well-made houses suggest that the living was a decent one. Each stocking maker had his own knitting frame, which he kept at home. The workrooms can be identified by the long windows, here on the first floor, which now light the sitting-rooms. Above and below were rooms for the family. Each house has a small yard at the back.

When we took them on, the roofs were falling in. We repaired the row of three, and gave one to the local preservation society to further its cause. You can stay in the other

two. No. 30 has been enlarged at some time, with a new stair and extra bedrooms. No. 32 still has its steep winding corner stair and a particularly fine view of the abbey from the top bedroom. Both cottages are light and cheerful, their upper floors looking out over the marvellous roofscape of Tewkesbury. St Mary's Lane itself runs down to the River Avon, on which there are still boatyards and other watery activities.

From the logbook
*We found ourselves so enchanted with Tewkesbury itself that we only ventured out on two days of the whole week.*

*Evensong every night.*

No.30

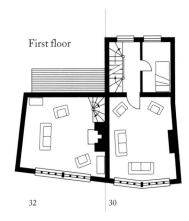

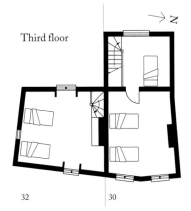

Ground floor    First floor    Second floor    Third floor

→ N

32    30    32    30    32    30    32    30

# St Winifred's Well

Woolston, near Oswestry, Shropshire

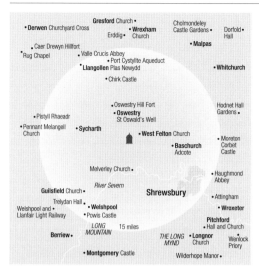

For up to 2 people
Solid fuel stove
Garden

Parking a short
walk away
Dogs allowed

St Winifred was a seventh century Welsh princess, sworn to a life of chastity, who was brought back to life by her uncle, St Beuno, after being decapitated by an angry suitor as she fled from him to take refuge in church. In the twelfth century her body was taken to Shrewsbury Abbey, where many pilgrims came to benefit from her healing miracles.

St Winifred was much loved in this area, so there is good reason to believe the tradition that this well at Woolston was dedicated to her; a lesser sister to the older and more famous St Winifred's Well at Holywell in Flintshire.

Whether it is true or not, the well here has been venerated for centuries, and is still visited by pilgrims. The innermost of the three pools is the medieval well chamber. The little building above is the medieval well chapel, itself a miraculous survival, preserved since the Reformation as a Court House and then as a cottage. Meanwhile, the well itself was enlarged to form a cold bath (your own hot, more private bath is a stone's throw from the cottage), first for a local squire, and later for the general public, whose conduct became so riotous that it was closed to them in 1755.

Thereafter it returned to nature, whose spirit was probably worshipped here long before Christianity. It is on the edge of a hamlet and hard to find (and rather harder to heat), approachable only by public footpath, which runs on, eventually, to a fragment of the old Shropshire Union Canal. Once here, acceptance of the miraculous is easy.

From the logbook
*Staying in a building that was built seven years before our country was discovered (Columbus 1492) is a unique experience.*

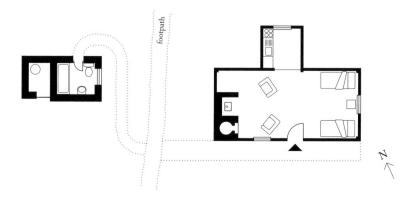

# Shelwick Court

Near Hereford, Herefordshire

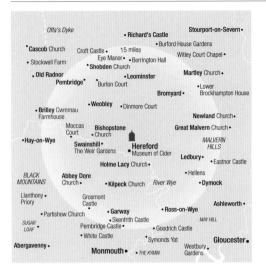

For up to 8 people
Solid fuel stove
Garden

Small pond in grounds
Adjacent parking
Dogs allowed

For many years this house had been falling down about the ears of an old farmer. It lies on the edge of a hamlet near Hereford, beside the long filled-in Gloucester & Hereford canal – made redundant, as so often, by the (still-active) railway and road built next to it.

Although it has a respectable stone front of about 1700, which with some difficulty we restrained from falling outwards, and a staircase of the same date, this alone would not have justified our intervention. But concealed within the house on the first floor, and indeed made almost invisible by later alterations, lies a medieval great chamber, with a six-bay open roof of massive timbers, cusped and chamfered in the Herefordshire manner.

What is more surprising still, this roof of about 1400 and the timber framing which

holds it up has clearly been moved here from somewhere else. It looks important enough to have been a hall, but there is no trace of smoke-blackening, and it must have formed, it seems, the solar cross-wing to a really grand hall, perhaps on a nearby site. Whatever its origins, it is a rare interior, which has, very strongly, a life of its own. This is a pleasure to share, even for a short time.

From the logbook
*We so enjoyed the house with its wonderfully comforting great hall.*

*We have spent a lot of time lying on the sofas, gazing up at the roof.*

*What a lovely space and what a pleasure to have so much of it.*

Ground floor

First floor

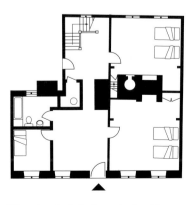

Stairs
to
attic

N
↑

There is a single bedroom in the attic.

# Shute Gatehouse

Near Axminster, Devon

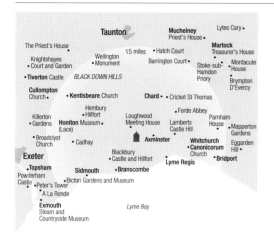

For up to 5 people
Solid fuel stove
Open grounds

Parking nearby
Dogs allowed

This gatehouse, which we lease from the National Trust, was probably built by William Pole when he bought Shute in about 1560. Then it led to a large medieval and Tudor house immediately behind, now much reduced in size and known as Shute Barton. When we first saw it, the gatehouse had mouldered picturesquely for some long time, its flues and fireplaces filled with sticks by jackdaws living in the immense elms around it. Much structural work was needed, but the weather has already begun to make what we did invisible.

While the repairs were being carried out North Devon District Council offered us a remarkable Jacobean plaster ceiling, from a house in Barnstaple demolished in the 1930s. The Council had been storing it in pieces ever since, but could do so no longer. Close in date to much of the gatehouse (which is not of a single date in any case), it fitted the upper room perfectly. So, although we would not usually do such a thing, we put it up and it looks wonderful.

The elms in front of the gatehouse, which were some of the best ever seen, succumbed to Dutch elm disease; but we took advantage of this calamity to restore the ground to its original level and lay it out as a green. As a result the gatehouse looks well from the village, and those who stay in it gain a fine view of the old deer-park, particularly from the kitchen sink.

## From the logbook
*The best part of the week? Seeing the gatehouse coming into view as we approached through the village, waking up to the cockerel crowing his head off in the mornings, feeling superior as people drive up to the gatehouse and get out looking impressed, hearing owls in Shute woods, and watching the bats.*

Second floor

The turret bedroom is spartan in character, with limited heating.

First floor

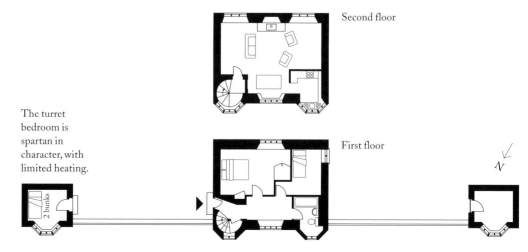

# South Street

Great Torrington, Devon

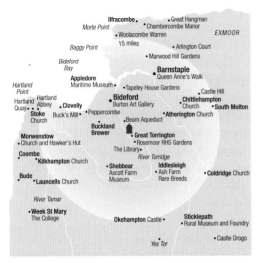

For up to 7 people
Open fire
Gas coal fire

Enclosed garden
Parking nearby
Dogs allowed

Giles Cawsey, merchant and Town Clerk, built this house in 1701. For nearly the first time in Devon, the main ground-floor rooms were designed for the family, instead of for trade. The panelled dining-room and the drawing-room are on either side of the front door, with a hall between leading to a fine staircase. The charm of the house lies not in its aspiration towards metropolitan high fashion, nor even in the long walled garden behind, but in the ceiling under which you can dine and the shell hood over the front door. One of Devon's most accomplished plasterers was employed to model crisp trophies of arms and musical instruments, amid foliage and stout mouldings.

Although long lived in by leading citizens, 28 South Street belonged to an ancient Town Lands charity. Recently used for offices, but deserving better, it was suggested to us by its Trustees. It offers the rare experience of living in a grand house in the street of an agreeable country town. Torrington, indeed, is very agreeable, settled on the top of one of North Devon's steep green hills. It has a weekly market, a good museum and enjoyable shops, whether you want fresh bread in the morning or locally made glass.

From the logbook
*The house is beautiful – we spent the first hour wandering from room to room, marvelling at the quality of workmanship and attention to detail.*

N

Ground floor

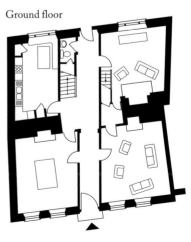

First floor

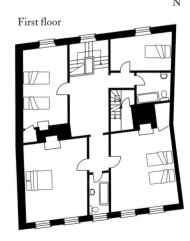

# The Steward's House

St Michael's Street, Oxford

For up to 2 people
Gas coal fire
No private parking

Oxford has more architectural pleasures and surprises than anywhere else in Britain, and nowhere else has so much spirit and energy been expended, often in marvellously silly ways. When, therefore, the Oxford Union Society needed money to repair their first debating chamber (now the library) we asked if, in return for a contribution, a place could be found where our visitors could stay.

The Union, formed as a debating society in 1823 to encourage free speech and speculation, acquired a site at No. 7 St Michael's Street in 1852. In 1856 their first debating chamber, which was to be a library as well, was built to the design of Benjamin Woodward, a disciple of Ruskin. While he was finishing the building he showed it to D. G. Rossetti and to William Morris, 'a rather rough and unpolished youth', and they offered to paint 'figures of some kind' in the gallery window bays – which they did in the Long Vacation, assisted by their friends, including Edward

Burne-Jones. William Morris finished his bay first and began painting the roof. These long-faded scenes from the Arthurian legend by famous painters in their youth, a wonderful possession for the Union, have been brought back to life, and the building restored.

In return for helping them we have a self-contained floor and a half in the former official residence of the Steward of the Union. He was an important, permanent figure who kept the show on the road, and kept order, while generations of undergraduates came and went. His spacious house was added, with a new library, in 1910 to the design of W. E. Mills of Oxford. It is a thoroughgoing Edwardian affair, of a kind and quality that we are pleased to look after; and our generously proportioned rooms, particularly the sitting-room, will give you a true impression of the Oxford of that day, while the vigorous and sometimes rather noisy activities of modern Oxford, and of the modern Union, take place around you.

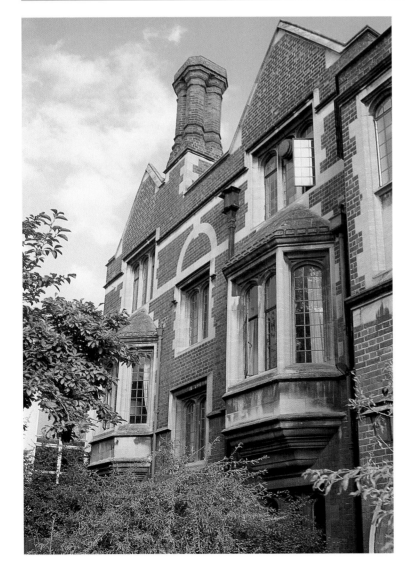

First floor

# Stockwell Farm

Old Radnor, Powys

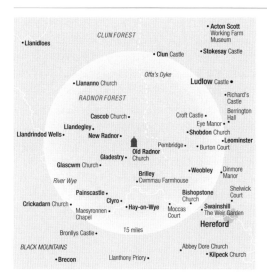

For up to 6 people
Open fire
Enclosed garden

Parking nearby
Steep staircase

Behind an unassuming farmhouse front, there is something rather earlier here, to which one old roof truss in a bedroom is the clue. This belongs to a house of about 1600, which had a sleeping loft above the main living-room and a door from the house to a cow byre (later a barn) under the same roof. At the other end a parlour wing was added in about 1700.

One of our visitors had been here long before, as a child evacuated from wartime London, and has left a moving account in the logbook: 'Missing are the neighbours who came to stare at the new children … Missing too the central fire, the cake hissing on the girdle … the hideous steamy Mondays … and the grisly boiled pig and tapioca'.

The house has a beautiful view; and behind are our own fields, into which you can turn your children, and across which you can walk up to Old Radnor. It is a particularly attractive hillside of rough pasture, full of mysterious hollows, green hummocks, ant-hills, thorn bushes and other unfunctional things. When the wind gets up, as it can in this exposed position, you can wrap up warm, gather round the fire and plan the next walk.

Old Radnor consists of a few scattered cottages, a fine fifteenth century church, containing the oldest organ case in Britain, and the Harp Inn, which we once owned and restored. Charles I is known to have been here since he complained about the food.

From the logbook
*We would love to return here: the lack of clutter is a pleasure to experience.*

*For botanists; there is a very good bog at Tregaron.*

*We have found Stockwell Farm charming … We would love to come again but it is a long way from Adelaide.*

*We have enjoyed the farm and the insight it gives one into the lives of our ancestors.*

Ground floor

Barn

First floor

Hay loft

Roof space

# Stogursey Castle

Stogursey, near Bridgwater, Somerset

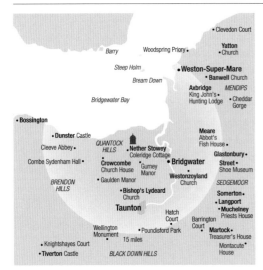

For up to 4 people
Open fire
Moated garden

Parking nearby
Dogs allowed

Stogursey, an old village to the east of the Quantocks, was chosen as his principal base by William de Courcy, Steward to Henry I. Both his son and his grandson married heiresses and the de Courcys became even more important. So, too, did their castle. Then the male line failed, and the castle was inherited by Alice de Courcy. She entertained King John here in 1210, when her husband won 20 shillings from him 'at play'.

Later on the Percys from Northumberland inherited it but, after a minor part in the Wars of the Roses, they could find no useful purpose for it as it stood and they did not think it worth rebuilding as a less fortified seat. So time and neglect, and adaptation to more humble uses, reduced it to ruins, in which it has lain ever since.

The small dwelling formed inside the gate towers of the castle has seventeenth-century roof timbers and was repaired in the 1870s; but when we found it, the entire castle had vanished beneath a mantle of vegetation. Clearing this and dredging the moat revealed an unsuspected thirteenth-century bridge. We also recovered some chain mail and other warlike fragments from the mud. The cottage makes a strange dwelling but a pleasant one, still commanding the only entrance to the castle's grassy inner ward, scene of all those doings long ago.

From the logbook
*Our daughters 7 and 6 lived a magical week in their moated castle.*

*Lots of local walks to do – no need to go further afield.*

A public footpath runs past the eastern end of the bridge.

Ground floor

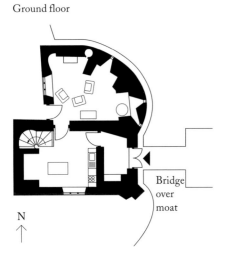

First floor

Bridge over moat

N

# Swarkestone Pavilion

Near Ticknall, Derbyshire

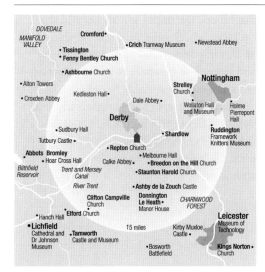

For up to 2 people
Enclosed garden

Roof terrace
Parking nearby

The excuse for building this majestic little pavilion was to give a grandstand view of whatever went on in the enclosure in front of it. Suggestions range from the romantic (jousting) and the rough (bear-baiting) to the more prosaic (bowls). Evidence supports the latter, with a payment in 1632 for a 'bowle alley house'. It was built by a mason, Richard Shepperd, but its design has been attributed to John Smythson, one of our first true architects and son of the great Robert. So, whatever its purpose, it is a building well worth preserving.

Swarkestone Hall was demolished by 1750. The pavilion survived, thanks to that most conserving of families, the Harpur Crewes of Calke, but it had long been a shell when we bought it. We re-roofed it and put back floors and windows, to recreate the room in which you live and sleep. The bathroom is in the top of one of the turrets, above the kitchen, and to reach it you must cross the open roof – an unlooked for opportunity to study the sky at night.

Swarkestone, with its important bridge across the Trent, has seen great events: a battle for its control in the Civil War did great damage to the Hall; and in 1745 it was the point at which Bonnie Prince Charlie recognised the futility of his attempt on the English throne and turned his troops back towards Scotland, to meet their fate at Culloden.

First floor

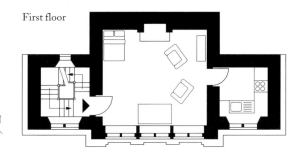

N

Second floor

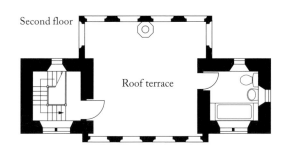

Roof terrace

# Tangy Mill

Kintyre, Argyll and Bute

For up to 6 people
Open fire
Open grounds

Adjacent parking
Steep staircase
Dogs allowed

Towards the southern end of Kintyre, on the western side, the landscape changes and there is a broad, open sweep of fertile land. Tangy Mill was built in about 1820, probably on the site of an earlier mill, to serve the big arable farms here. It stands in beautiful remote surroundings on the north bank of the Tangy Burn, near the point where it enters the sea, and is made of harled whinstone with sandstone dressings. For our repairs we obtained more of this sandstone from the original quarry.

Because of the climate (which often merits extra layers of clothing) the grain, mostly oats, had to be dried before grinding, and there is a two-storey kiln with a big revolving ventilator, known as a 'granny', on its roof. Here the oats were spread six inches deep on the perforated iron floor of what is now one of the bedrooms. When we bought the mill, the dressing, drying, hoisting and grinding machinery, the stones and shutes and the backshot wheel, were still there; we have kept all this in position and amongst it you live and sleep. The atmosphere of old places of work is almost impossible to preserve, because one cannot preserve old workmen and old ways of life; but this mill was so complete and in such an unexpected place that here for once, changing as little as possible, we have attempted it.

From the logbook
*Delicious lobsters can be bought from fishermen near the Tourist Office in Campbeltown.*

*We saw dolphins off the beach. There was a whole group of them going quite fast, leaping through the water – it was magical.*

*We can hardly believe we've seen the Irish Sea, Atlantic Ocean, Ireland, seals, swans in the sea, a golden eagle, jellyfish, peacocks, palm trees, etc etc.*

Ground floor

First floor

There are two further beds in the loft.

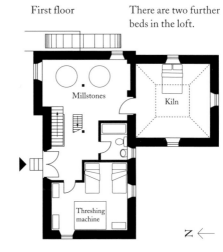

# Tixall Gatehouse

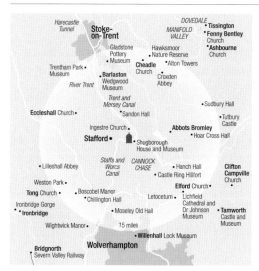

For up to 6 people
Roof terrace
Small fenced garden
Steep spiral staircase

Adjacent parking
for 2 cars
Dogs allowed

Tixall Gatehouse was built in about 1580 by Sir Walter Aston to stand in front of an older house. This house and a successor, built in 1780, have disappeared, and the gatehouse today is surrounded by grass. It was described in 1598 as 'one of the fairest pieces of work made of late times in all these counties' and, more recently, as 'an Elizabethan ruin, without roof, floors or windows, used as a shelter for cattle'.

Mary, Queen of Scots, was imprisoned at Tixall for two weeks in 1586. Her son James I came here once for two days. In 1678 the Aston of the day was sent briefly to the Tower, accused of a part in the Titus Oates conspiracy. A century later, his descendant Thomas Clifford, guided by 'the celebrated Brown' and his pupil Eames, ingeniously made use of a new canal to form a lake in his park – known to boaters as Tixall Wide.

We bought the gatehouse for £300 in 1968. On its first floor we made five large rooms, one of them a gallery with an oriel window at each end above the two archways. In the spandrels of these archways are, facing the outside world, armed warriors; and on the inside, voluptuous ladies thinly disguised as angels.

The roof is paved with stone, and to be high up here among the balustrades and turret tops, with Arcadian landscape on every side, is an important Landmark Trust experience. The gatehouse clock lives in one of the turrets (as do two bracing cabin-like bedrooms and the bathrooms); this strikes the hour, and perhaps the half hour, but has no hands or face to show the actual time, which seems unimportant here, even vulgar.

First floor

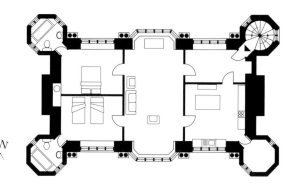

There are two small
single bedrooms and a
bathroom in the turrets
on the second floor.

# The Tower, Canons Ashby

Northamptonshire

For up to 3 people
Garden
Roof terrace

Parking nearby
Steep spiral staircase

There can be few houses in which every detail, inside and out, is pleasing to look at, but this can truly be claimed of Canons Ashby. The last time it was altered in any major way was in 1710. Thereafter, its intelligent and sensitive owners, the Drydens, matched their tastes and needs to those of their house. Early decoration lives happily with later furniture, all of the greatest charm and interest.

In 1980 the house was transferred to the National Trust, after a public appeal. We contributed to the restoration fund and offered to pay for the creation and repair of one flat. Accordingly we were given the top of the sixteenth-century tower, where there were formerly two bedrooms, reached by a newel stair with solid oak treads. We tidied up these light and pleasant rooms, which look down the axis of the slowly reviving garden, and put a bathroom and kitchen in two adjoining attics. A new dormer window was made to light the kitchen, which is invisible from below but provides an agreeable roofscape to look at from the sink.

Meanwhile, the quiet building below has come back to life, and is opened to the public by the National Trust, normally from April to October – and to you, free of charge, within opening times when you stay here. On the top of the tower you have your own hidden refuge, and at the end of the day, when the last visitor has gone, you can enjoy the privilege of an owner and walk in the garden undisturbed.

Second floor

Tower room

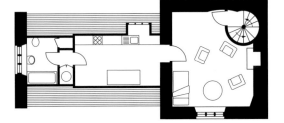

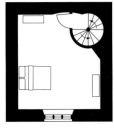

# Tower Hill

St David's, Pembrokeshire

This house occupies a most important site. It is built just above the close wall at St David's and has an astonishing view of the cathedral, facing it squarely at tower level. To arrive here is to feel that you have completed a pilgrimage, drawn down the long Pembrokeshire peninsula towards a place of worship that was already ancient when the Normans built their cathedral beside it. There is still much of the monastery here, in the actual buildings that survive, in their sense of enclosure within the valley and in the warmth of their welcome when finally you top the last hill, and pass between the last houses, to obtain your first full view of them.

The living-room, too, has great serenity, with the sun on one side and the sunlit cathedral on the other. Here little need

trouble you, and at your door is the reassurance of cathedral life, its services, the bells and the building itself. The sea is about a mile away in most directions; the coastal path, with stunning views, encircles St David's – 'a long way, but very good for you'.

From the logbook
*Tower Hill has its own elevating appeal.*

*We arrived in the dark and were absolutely knocked out the following morning when we opened the curtains to the view of the Cathedral.*

For up to 6 people
Open fire
Enclosed garden

Parking nearby
Dogs allowed

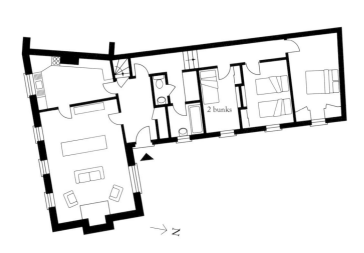

2 bunks

# Warden Abbey

Old Warden, Bedfordshire

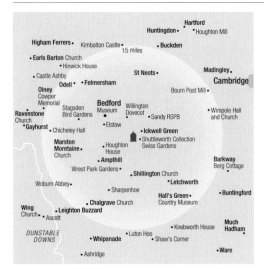

For up to 5 people
Open fire
Small fenced garden
Parking a short walk
away across a field

Steep spiral staircase
Dogs allowed

Warden Abbey was Cistercian, founded in 1135. It was dissolved in 1537 and a large house was built on the site by the Gostwick family. The seal of the abbey on the deed of surrender bears St Mary with the infant Christ standing on her knee. On the counter-seal is a crozier between three Warden pears.

Nothing remains of house or abbey above ground except this puzzling fragment, of which we have a long lease. It stands near a big farm, in a meadow made uneven by what lies underneath, and is an extremely perplexing building of very high quality. Clearly it formed part of the Gostwicks' house, but it also incorporates part of the abbey; in the course of our repairs a fourteenth-century tile pavement emerged, one of the finest ever discovered, which you can see for yourselves in Bedford Museum.

The principal room downstairs seems to have been part of a gallery or broad corridor, with a large open fireplace added to one end.

Occupying the entire first floor is a single room with a Tudor fireplace, an oriel window and a heavily moulded oak ceiling. It is a pleasure to lie here in bed and wonder for whom such a splendid room can have been constructed: for one of the last abbots, for his guests, or for the Gostwicks? Above is a superb attic, in which one visitor put her three aunts, uproariously sharing a room for the first time since childhood.

The surrounding country has had the advantage of belonging to large estates and is some of the best in Bedfordshire.

From the logbook
*A fantastic retreat from the rigours of life in a large city. Peaceful, serene, and with the perfect company, a most romantic environment.*

*When reading the history album supplied by Landmark, people become flesh and blood in a way that no history lesson at school could create.*

Ground floor

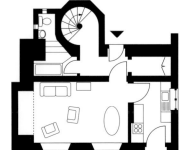

First floor

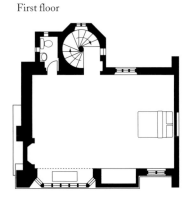

Attic floor

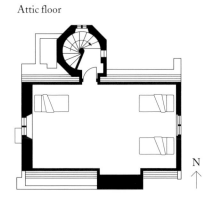

N ↑

# The Wardrobe

The Cathedral Close, Salisbury, Wiltshire

For up to 4 people
Gas coal fire
Garden

Parking nearby
Access by steep
staircase

In return for our help with rehousing their museum in the Wardrobe (which had been empty for some time and needed expensive repairs), the Berkshire and Wiltshire Regiment allowed us to form a flat high up in the attics. Here, approached by a seventeenth-century staircase, are three lofty rooms, each with a different outlook. The Landmark prides itself on the views from its many windows, but the view from the sitting-room here of the cathedral is one of the best of all, whether by day or by night, when it seems to be floodlit expressly for one's benefit.

The Wardrobe, which contains traces of a substantial medieval hall, was once the Bishop's storehouse, and so got its name. It has been a house since before 1600, mostly let by the Dean and Chapter to laymen, who formed in it some very handsome rooms, now part of the museum. One family, the Husseys, must have used our attics as a nursery, since during our building work we discovered toys,

and even a manuscript novel by a 13 year old Victorian daughter.

All cathedral closes have a special quality, but this is one of the very best, a succession of beautiful houses ranged round the only English cathedral built at one go. Behind the Wardrobe a long walled garden, which those who stay here may use, runs down to the swift and silent Avon.

From the logbook
*We climbed the stairs and the Cathedral became ours for a week – choirs rehearsing evensong, the doves, the laughter of children on the green, the sound of cricket bats, bells ringing the changes … just listen.*

*A must is to read Golding's 'The Spire', then go on the roof tour of the Cathedral.*

*Even on the short journey from bedroom to bathroom I could not resist a detour to make sure the view was still there.*

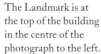

The Landmark is at the top of the building in the centre of the photograph to the left.

Second floor

# West Blockhouse

Dale, Pembrokeshire

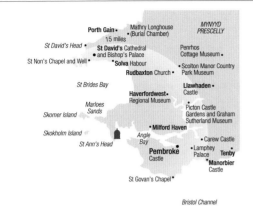

This is the outermost work of the mid-nineteenth-century fortification of Milford Haven. It had a single battery of six heavy guns commanding the entrance to the harbour, with defensible barracks behind to give protection from attack on the landward side. The fort was completed in 1857 and contained accommodation for a garrison of 34 men and one officer. It continued in use until after the Second World War, updated from time to time with new guns and new emplacements.

The walls of finely dressed limestone are of exceptional quality (as too were the repairs to them). The size of the granite coping stones on the parapet of the battery itself will astonish even those familiar with Victorian ideas of how a job should be done. The Victorians also knew how to make themselves comfortable: inside, the rooms on the first floor are lined with thick pine boards so that, with the coal fire burning, you are cosily remote from the elements.

It is a vertiginous spot, but the view down the coast of Pembrokeshire is one to savour. Victorian fortification and more recent industry alike are dwarfed and absorbed. There is still, occasionally, the spectacle of a big ship feeling her way into the mouth of the haven at one's feet. In contrast, there is a sheltered, south-facing beach within a few hundred yards.

From the logbook
*What a building, what a history and what a weekend.*

For up to 8 people
Open fire
Roof platform
Parking a short
walk by steep footpath

External staircases
and drawbridge
Dogs allowed

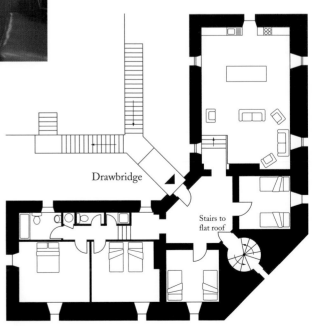

First floor

Drawbridge

Stairs to
flat roof

# The White House

Aston Munslow, Shropshire

For up to 8 people     Adjacent parking
Open fire     Dogs allowed
Large garden

This was long the home of Miss Constance Purser, who nurtured it and uncovered its past, building up a collection of household and agricultural implements, and opened it to the public in a small way. In 1990 she passed the house and its contents on to us.

Until 1945 the White House belonged to the Stedmans, who had lived here from soon after 1300 in a nearly unbroken line. The tops of the great cruck trusses of their hall can be seen in the roof space. Below are rooms of Tudor and Jacobean date, with wide uneven oak floorboards and a pleasing jumble of different windows. After a fire in 1780, a polite new drawing-room was added at one end, with a bedroom above.

The house stands on the south side of Wenlock Edge, and the garden runs down the hill in front, with long views of Corvedale towards Ludlow, capital of the Marches. Just below is the village of Aston Munslow. Behind the house are outbuildings of all shapes and dates and sizes, many containing equipment appropriate to their original use.

From the logbook
*The sheep grazing on the hill, the smell of the farm crops, the silent and restful ambience of this wonderful old house.*

*We took a tarpaulin on to the lawn and lay on our backs to watch the shooting stars.*

Ground floor

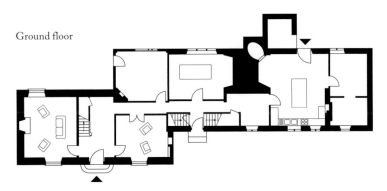

First floor

N
↑

# Whiteford Temple

Near Callington, Cornwall

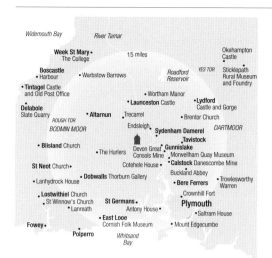

For up to 2 people
Open fire

Small garden
Adjacent parking

The Duchy of Cornwall generously gave us this handsome granite building. It was put up in 1799 for Sir John Call, a military engineer who had made a fortune in India. By 1770, at the age of 38, he was able to retire, marry and build himself a substantial mansion. This, with the estate, was sold to the Duchy in 1879. The house was largely demolished in 1913, and today all that remains are traces of its garden, part of the stables, and this temple, on its own, high above.

It is not clear how it was reached from the house, how its surroundings were laid out, nor how it was used – though its three arches were certainly glazed at one time. Accounts of a party held in it in 1847 make one suppose that it must then have been larger;

and also that it was nearer to the house, so perhaps it has been moved. It had become a shelter for cattle when we first saw it, with a roof of corrugated iron and a floor of earth.

It has a fine open view, looking towards the estuary of the Tamar in the distance; and it is well designed, an ornament in the landscape which it would be sad to lose. Accordingly, we restored it, as a single large room with two small wings, which is our best guess at what its unknown architect intended.

From the logbook
*What a room with a view.*

*The temple is a pleasure worth waiting for.*

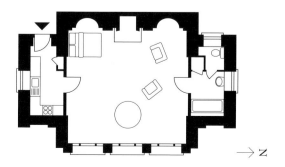

→ N

# Wilmington Priory

Wilmington, near Eastbourne, East Sussex

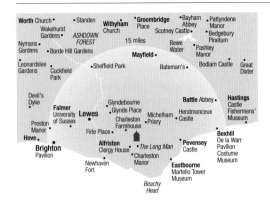

Wilmington Priory was a cell of the Benedictine Abbey at Grestain in Normandy. Never a conventional priory with cloister and chapter, the monks prayed in the adjoining parish church, where the thousand-year old yews are testimony to the age of the site. The Priory has been added to and altered in every age, some of it has been lost to ruin and decay, but what is left shows how highly it was once regarded.

Staying here you will have the benefit of enjoying the medieval site with its fine vaulted entrance porch, mullioned window in the wall of the ruined Great Chamber, and stair turrets, combined with the comfort of living in rooms improved by the Georgians. Add to that the sense of adventure as you make your way to bed in the first floor medieval porch bedroom, through the attic with its open cathedral-like roof and tracery,

and, once there, look out at the Long Man in this peaceful, unchanged landscape.

From this ancient place you can go to the opera at Glyndebourne, admire the work of the Bloomsbury group or perhaps go bucket and spading in Eastbourne. Whatever you choose, Wilmington itself with its agreeable village street, pub, and downland walks, all overlooked by the famous Long Man, has much to offer.

From the logbook
*To be in Wilmington is to be intoxicated by history.*

*It's nice having a kitchen big enough to waltz in and no doubt polka if we only knew how.*

*The grounds and occasionally the building are open to the public by appointment, but this is most unlikely to happen while the building is occupied.*

For up to 6 people
Open fire
Enclosed garden

Parking nearby
Dogs allowed

Ground floor

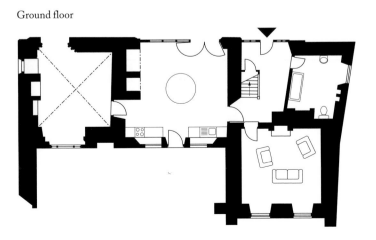

First floor

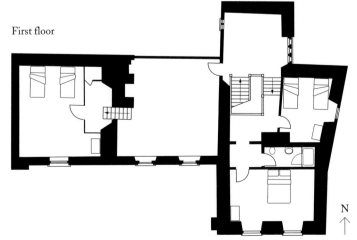

N

# Wolveton Gatehouse

For up to 6 people
Open fire
Garden

Parking nearby
Spiral staircase
Uneven drive

Dorset families did well under the Tudors, and many passed their good fortune on to us in the houses they built. The Trenchards of Wolveton, in the water meadows west of Dorchester, put up one of the finest. John Trenchard inherited Wolveton through his mother, Christian Mohun, in 1480 and began work on the house. Sir Thomas Trenchard completed the Gatehouse in the reign of Henry VIII. Most of Sir Thomas's house was demolished in the 1820s, leaving the lavish Elizabethan wing, erected by Sir George Trenchard. What remains is exceptional: windows with the delicate decoration of the Tudor Renaissance, an Elizabethan display of glass and much moulded oak and plaster.

The present owner opens his home to the public and has also repaired and furnished the Gatehouse, which we now let on his behalf. On two of its corners are twin towers from an earlier fortified gatehouse. Thought to be fourteenth century, each has a dovecot in its top. The two rooms on the first floor were, and still are, fitted out for guests. They are reached by a wide and ancient spiral stair in which newel post and tread are carved of single blocks, not of stone but of oak. Both have Jacobean fireplaces, and turret rooms leading off them. A garret above and the guardroom below provide extra bedrooms. In winter, stoke up the fire and wear an extra layer, as the Dorset nobility would have done hundreds of years ago.

The Gatehouse once framed the approach to a grand forecourt and the great of many kinds have passed through it. Today it reminds us of the noble house that Wolveton once was. Thomas Hardy came to tea at Wolveton in 1900 and the tragic tale of Lady Penelope D'Arcy, the second wife of George Trenchard, appears in his book of short stories, *A Group of Noble Dames*.

*Wolveton House (not the Gatehouse) is open to the public during the summer.*

Ground floor

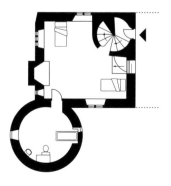

→ N

First floor

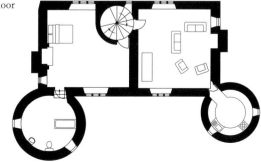

Second floor

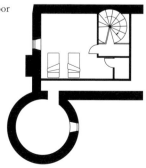

# Woodsford Castle

Near Dorchester, Dorset

For up to 8 people
Open fire
Garden
Parking nearby

Dogs allowed
Steep staircases
Outside steps
without railings

All that remains here is one side of a quadrangular castle, licensed in 1335 and completed in about 1370. The grand apartment and lesser lodgings that make up the existing building were almost certainly the work of Sir Guy de Bryan KG, a close friend and servant of King Edward III, who bought the castle in 1367. Defence is just beginning to give way to a more domestic way of life; but although the hall and the chapel next to it have large windows in the outer walls, they are still up on the first floor, over vaulted kitchens and store rooms.

When we acquired the castle it had passed by inheritance for over 600 years. Two of its owners, the Earls of Ormonde and Devon, were executed in succession during the Wars of the Roses. It then went by marriage to the Strangways, fell into decay and became a farmhouse – an enormous roof of thatch replacing the original turrets and crenellations. Meanwhile, the other three sides of the castle gradually disappeared, their stone put to more useful purpose elsewhere.

Inside, among much other work, we have restored the King's Room, or hall, and given it a new oak ceiling. This, with the chapel and the adjoining Queen's Room, form the main rooms in which you will stay; their size could justify bringing an extra jersey in the winter. The kitchen, and more bedrooms, are in a warmer eighteenth-century wing on the north-west corner.

An earlier restoration in 1850 was carried out by the builder father of Thomas Hardy, and Hardy himself came here often. It is indeed a prime spot for those who like his books. The castle stands on the south bank of the Frome, three miles below Dorchester, and the north window of the hall looks out across the river and water meadows to the high ground of Egdon Heath. All this is his stage; here Hardy's characters act out their narrow parts, against a backdrop of the Universe.

First floor

There is a second bathroom on the ground floor.

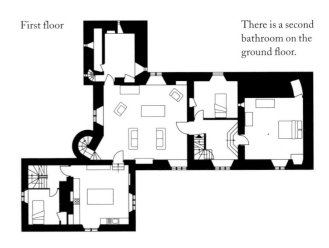

Second floor

Upper part of Hall

# Woodspring Priory

Near Weston-Super-Mare, Somerset

For up to 8 people
Open fire
Parking for 3 cars

Spiral staircase
Dogs allowed

Woodspring Priory was founded in 1210, perhaps as an expiatory gesture, by William de Courtenay, grandson of Reginald FitzUrse who, with other West Countrymen, murdered Thomas à Becket. It was an Augustinian house of the rare Victorine rule, and had St Thomas the Martyr as a patron saint.

The priory was a small one but, as elsewhere in Somerset, flourished in the fifteenth century, when the tower and nave of the church, the infirmary and a great barn were built of a beautiful golden stone. The north aisle was unfinished when, in 1536, the priory was suppressed and the church, most unusually, turned into a house, a chimney-stack built up through the roof of the nave.

We found Woodspring in 1969 as it had been since the Dissolution, the church still inhabited as the farmhouse of a picturesque and rather old-fashioned farm. However, the buildings had suffered greatly from the ravages of time. We repaired the church tower (one man and a boy, using ladders) and reinstated the crossing and north aisle inside it. These and the infirmary are open to the public (daylight hours, all year round).

The rest of the priory, including the range built in 1701 on the site of the prior's lodging, we have repaired for you to stay in. Two bedrooms and the sitting-room occupy the nave of the church, each containing some token of its ecclesiastical past. Their windows look south on to walled gardens, once the cloister and outer court.

Other monastic remains are grander, others more complete than Woodspring, but few have kept so well the serene atmosphere of an isolated religious community, surrounded by a working farm, and lying by the sea.

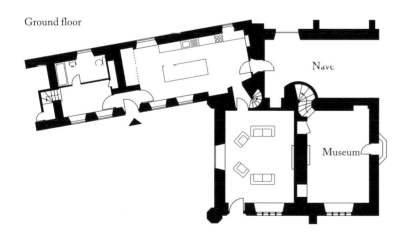

Ground floor

Nave

Museum

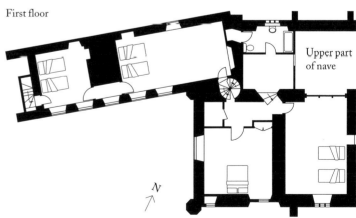

First floor

Upper part
of nave

N

# Wortham Manor

Lifton, Devon

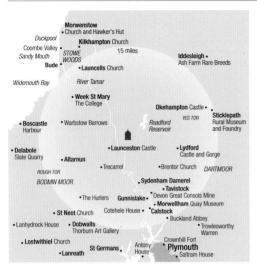

For up to 15 people
Open fire
Enclosed garden
Parking nearby

Some steep staircases
Large millpond
nearby
Dogs allowed

This is a medieval and Tudor house of the highest quality, built and then remodelled by a junior branch of the great Devon family of Dinham, but little altered since. Doors and windows are of finely dressed granite, a noble if intractable material seen to great advantage here.

The chamber over the hall has an open arch-braced roof, less massive but otherwise very like that in the great hall at Cotehele, further down the Tamar valley. The hall itself has a ceiling of heavily moulded oak beams and rich late Gothic carving. Both are close in date, and may even have been put up together soon after 1500. Together with the carved surround of the front door, they are probably the work of John Dinham, cousin of Dame Thomasine of Week St Mary, whose building work at The College (see page 45)

he oversaw. Like her, he had lived, and prospered, in London. In 1533, when an old man, he was pressed to take a knighthood, but declined.

Along with much other work, the house had to be entirely re-roofed, which gave us the opportunity to recover its original plan. We also bought some of the farm buildings on two sides of the house so that its setting could be preserved as well. Those who stay here have an unrivalled opportunity to experience the life of a prosperous, and quite sophisticated, Tudor gentleman, in that distant part of Devon once known as Cornwall in England.

From the logbook
*Ran around like children choosing rooms. Still can't believe this is our home for a few days.*

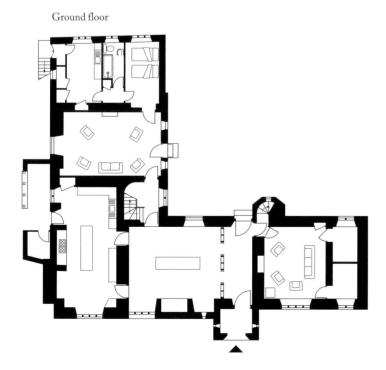

Ground floor

First floor

N

Lundy Island

# Lundy Island

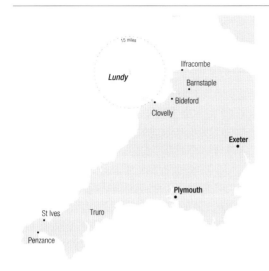

23 houses and cottages, including a castle and a lighthouse.

Lundy ('Puffin Island'), in the approaches to the Bristol Channel, is three miles long and rises over 400 feet out of the sea, commanding a tremendous view of England, Wales and the Atlantic. It has tall cliffs towards the south and west, with grass and heather on top, and steep side lands with trees, shrubs and bracken in small hanging valleys, rich in wildflowers, on the east coast facing the mainland. There are three lighthouses (two in use), a castle, a church, an active farm, a pub, several handsome houses and cottages, and a population of about 18. Most of the buildings and all the field walls are made of the island's beautiful light-coloured granite.

When Lundy was taken on by the National Trust in 1969 (thanks mainly to the generosity of Sir Jack Hayward), we undertook to restore and run the island. The formidable task of tidying up and restoring the buildings and services for both visitors and residents took us over 20 years. Much of this work remains invisible, but without it, ordinary people would soon have been unable to live on or visit the island.

Lundy offers the public a very rare experience. It is large enough to have a genuine life of its own, which visitors can share and enjoy, but small and far enough away to be a world apart and undefaced. It offers both the pleasures of escape and the pleasures of participation: walks or wanderings high up, in the silence, looking east across the blue floor of the sea to the coast of Devon, or westward over the limitless Atlantic; or sociable visits to the tavern and shop.

# Lundy Island

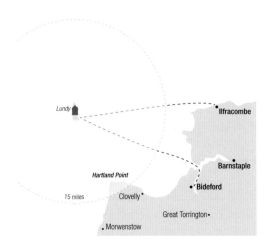

Opportunities abound for field studies of all kinds; and for the energetic there is rock climbing, or diving and snorkelling in the Marine Nature Reserve. Everybody has the free run of the whole island, and it is surprising how much out of the ordinary there is to do and see at all times of the year.

Our handsome supply ship, the *MS Oldenburg*, runs between March and November from Bideford or Ilfracombe, carrying day and staying visitors, weather permitting. Between November and March a helicopter transfers visitors between the mainland and the island from Hartland Point. On the island we have made it possible to stay at various levels of price and comfort – in cottages, in a hostel, or by camping – so that almost anyone can afford to be here. Your arrival on the island is an event. To come here, even for the day, is a small adventure. All those who experience the space and light, the life of the island, and the natural beauty on every hand, have thereafter something in common which they treasure.

*If you would like to know more, we can send you our free, full colour guide to staying on Lundy.*

Old
Light

Stoneycroft

The Barn
The Quarters

Shop
and
Tavern

Millcombe House

Old House

Government House

Radio Room

Old School

Square Cottage

Bramble Villa

St Johns

Hanmers

Castle

# Lundy Island

## The Barn

The Barn, which was roofless when we arrived, is now a hostel, at the centre of island life. The dormitory rooms are lined with varnished wood; it has a large living-room with a big open fire and, from the sleeping gallery, one of the best views on the island.

For up to 14 people
Open fire
Shower only

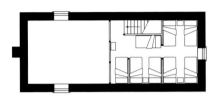

First floor

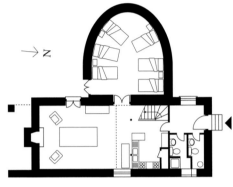

→ N

Ground floor

## Bramble Villa

Bramble Villa is in the St John's Valley, on the site of a ruinous corrugated iron building of the same name, and the same rather colonial appearance. It was shipped, ready made, from the mainland, and put up to house those who were to carry out the restoration work for us on Lundy. Now divided in two, East looks over the sea towards Devon and has the light off the sea in its rooms. West also has a glimpse of the sea, but is more sheltered.

Bramble Villa East
For up to 4 people
Solid fuel stove

Bramble Villa West
For up to 4 people
Solid fuel stove

West                              East

# The Castle

The Castle was built by Henry III in about 1250, and paid for by the sale of rabbits. High up on the south-east point of the island, it replaced the earlier castle of the unruly Mariscos, which stood in Bull's Paradise behind the farm. In the Civil War Lundy was held for the Royalists to the very end by Thomas Bushell, who rebuilt the castle. He owned a silver mine and tradition says he minted coins here.

By 1787 cottages had been built round the small courtyard inside the Keep. These have decayed and been rebuilt several times, most recently by us, as three Castle Keep Cottages. They are snug and sociable, inward-looking except for one or two windows in the outer walls which have spectacular marine views.

Castle Keep East
For up to 2 people
Shower only
Solid fuel stove

Castle Keep South
For up to 4 people
Shower only
Solid fuel stove

Castle Keep North
For up to 2 people
Shower only
Solid fuel stove

Castle Keep East

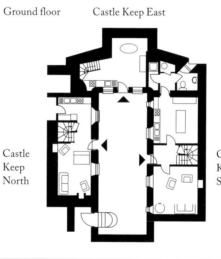

Ground floor    Castle Keep East

First floor    Castle Keep East

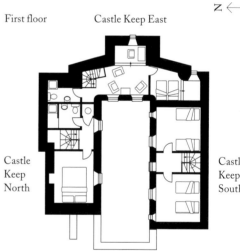

# Castle Cottage

Castle Cottage, built on to the outside of the Keep, is the old post office and cable station, with an addition made by the Harman family. It does not improve the look of the castle, but it makes such a good place to spend a holiday, with a wonderful view, that we have not had the heart to demolish it.

For up to 2 people
Shower only

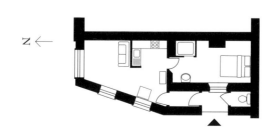

# Lundy Island

## Government House

Government House was designed by Philip Jebb to house whoever runs the island, and to make use of and preserve the fine granite dressings left when additions to Old House were removed. However, our agents since have unselfishly preferred to remain in humbler quarters, and so it is available for you to stay in. It is one of the best houses we possess, and so well sited that it seems always to have been there, sheltered on three sides and looking down the Millcombe valley towards the sea.

For up to 5 people
Open fire

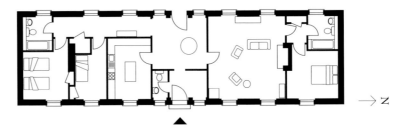

## Hanmers

Hanmers was built by a fisherman in 1902. He chose a good site, a dip in the hill, on the path from the beach to the castle, so the place is sheltered but has the usual wonderful view out to sea towards Devon. It is weather-boarded outside and its interior is also of wood, painted white in the front rooms, which gives it a warm and solid feel.

For up to 4 people
Shower only
Solid fuel stove

# Millcombe House

Millcombe House was built in 1836 for the Heaven family, looking down a wooded valley and out to sea. Most of the furniture in its well-proportioned rooms is also nineteenth-century, and some of the pictures are very interesting. The curious inward-sloping roof, which we have restored to its original form, was designed to catch rainwater.

For up to 12 people
Solid fuel stove

Ground floor

First floor

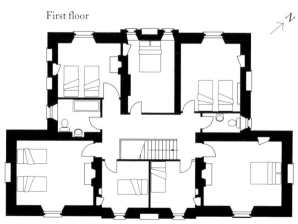

# Lundy Island

## Old House

Old House, North and South, is the most handsome building on the island, in perhaps the best position, and made of the best-looking granite. It began life in about 1775, built for Sir John Borlase Warren, a young MP who owned Lundy briefly. Until replaced by Millcombe it was indeed the island's chief residence. William Heaven gave it its present form, to which it has now returned after the removal, by us, of haphazard additions on three sides. We also made a garden in the courtyard behind and divided the house, invisibly, in two.

Old House North
For up to 2 people
Solid fuel stove

Old House South
For up to 5 people
Open fire

The interior of Old House South *right*.

Old House *below*.

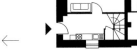
Old House North
Ground floor

Old House South

Old House North
First floor

Old House South

z ←

# Old Light

Old Light, completed in 1820, was designed by Daniel Asher Alexander. Built of Cyclopean blocks of granite, it stands on the highest point of the island. The keepers' quarters are still divided into the two original flats, Lower and Upper, very satisfying in design and detail. Unusually for Lundy, they look out over the northern part of the island.

Old Light Lower
For up to 4 people
Solid fuel stove
Shower only

Old Light Upper
For up to 5 people
Solid fuel stove
Shower only

Old Light Lower

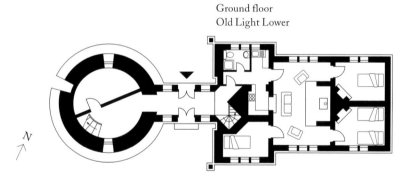

Ground floor
Old Light Lower

First floor
Old Light Upper

# Old Light Cottage

Old Light Cottage was the lighthouse keepers' store, solidly built of granite to the usual Trinity House standard. We have equipped it, and the Radio Room near the Tavern, for those who come to Lundy on their own. It stands in the same compound as the Old Light, and has in it just about everything that one person can want.

For 1 person
Shower only

# Lundy Island

## Old School

Old School, long known as 'the Blue Bung', lies near St John's Cottages and shares much the same outlook. It is a small building of corrugated iron, with a snug interior lined with match boarding. Designed and made with care, in better times, it has, like many such buildings, considerable point and charm.

For up to 2 people
Shower only

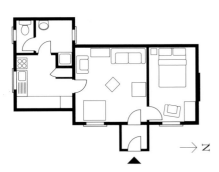

→ N

## The Quarters

The Quarters is the name traditionally given to the long wooden buildings, one behind the other, which were originally put up to house teams of builders on the island. The Landmark within the Quarters has recently been improved: moved to the end of the block and refurbished to a higher standard than the previous accommodation. Sleeping fewer than before, the Quarters has the feel of a cottage: you can now have a bath here and sit in your own enclosed garden, while still enjoying that fine view of the church and beyond to Hartland Point.

For up to 5 people
Solid fuel stove

N
↑

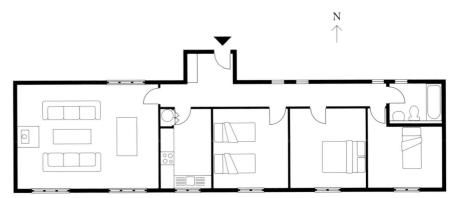

## Radio Room

The Radio Room is a small solid building in the walled garden behind Old House. It used to house the ancient wireless transmitter with which for many years the island kept in touch with the mainland. It is cosy and self-contained, with an east-facing terrace.

For 1 person
Shower only

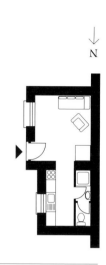

## St John's

Big and Little St John's are a pair of single storey cottages, added by the Harman family to an existing granite barn in the St John's valley. Although they are not the most handsome buildings on the island, they are two of the best loved. They occupy a fine position, sheltered and secluded, with a beautiful view towards Devon.

Big St John's
For up to 3 people
Shower only

Little St John's
For up to 2 people
Shower only

Little St John's

Big St John's                    Little St John's

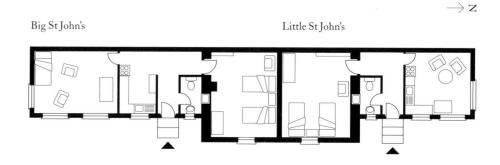

# Lundy Island

## Square Cottage

Square Cottage was formed by us from the remains of the nineteenth-century quarry manager's house. Its front door opens on to the garden behind Old House, but to south and east it has spectacular views, especially from the upstairs sitting-room, which has a good Victorian fireplace. It also has central heating, using up surplus energy from the island's generator, and is very comfortable in winter.

For up to 3 people
Solid fuel stove

First floor

Ground floor

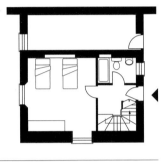

## Stoneycroft

Stoneycroft was where the lighthouse inspectors stayed when they visited Lundy. It stands in its own walled enclosure, near the Old Light, facing south.

For up to 4 people
Enclosed garden
Solid fuel stove
Shower only

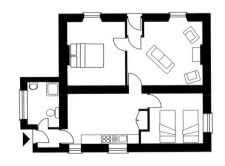

N

# Tibbetts

Tibbetts was built of pale granite to a functional and satisfying design, in 1909, on the second highest point of the island. It is about 1¾ miles from the village along the main track to the north, and is as remote and simple as anyone could wish. It is said that 14 lighthouses can be seen from it on a clear night. The interior is lined with varnished matchboarding and keeps its original purposeful atmosphere because of its distance from the village. Tibbetts is the only property that has no electricity; however it has a pumped water supply and a shower. It also retains the original four built-in bunks and is the sort of place where you can wander around in your pyjamas collecting mushrooms for breakfast.

For up to 4 people
Solid fuel stove
Shower only
Gas lighting
No electricity

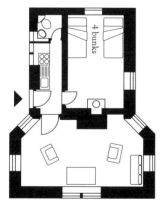

Italy

Casa Guidi, Florence

Italian culture has had a profound effect on the British, from the days of the Roman Empire, through the Renaissance and that institution for young aristocratic tourists known as the Grand Tour, to the Romantic poets of the nineteenth century. The revival of Classical architecture, so prevalent in the country seats of our own eighteenth-century gentry, found initial inspiration in Andrea Palladio's *Quattro Libri dell'Architettura*, based on close study of the ruins of antiquity that lay everywhere around, and the most important architectural treatise of the Renaissance.

On this basis then, it becomes less surprising to encounter the following handful of carefully selected Italian Landmarks in this Handbook, all of which have some connection with British culture, which has always been a guiding principle in our selection of Landmarks abroad. If you have stayed in other Landmarks, you will find much that is familiar in our Italian buildings, and here the beauty of both the Italian landscape and its climate lie just outside your door.

Sant'Antonio *top*, Piazza di Spagna *left* and Villa Saraceno *above*.

# Casa Guidi

Piazza S. Felice, Florence

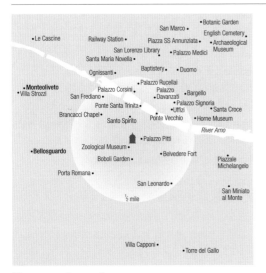

For up to 6 people
No private parking

Pen Browning, son of the poets Elizabeth and Robert, wished his parents' Florentine home, in which they had spent nearly all the happy and productive years of their marriage, to be recreated in their memory. He did not live to see his wish fulfilled, but it was remembered.

In 1971 the suite of rooms on the first floor of the Palazzo Guidi was acquired by the Browning Institute. Restoration began, with the eventual aim of refurnishing the drawing-room, a romantic literary sanctum recorded by the painter Mignaty after Elizabeth's death in 1861. The familiar writer's clutter of books and paper-burdened tables was here given a grand setting, of richly carved furniture and Renaissance paintings, mingled with comfortable sofas and armchairs, all bought by the Brownings with the excitement of a young married couple.

Casa Guidi is now owned by Eton College and leased to us. Parties of boys undergo its civilising influence at intervals but at all other times it is available for our visitors. The tall main rooms, with graceful eighteenth-century decoration, are furnished much as they were by the two poets. Like them, and like their many guests, you can savour the agreeable and busy streets of Florence through Casa Guidi's windows.

From the logbook

*Having come to Florence before as a mere tourist it was wonderful to come to Casa Guidi and really feel part of the place.*

*It has been a week of sheer cultural enrichment; surrounded by Browning anthologies we were able to continue indulging long after the museums and palazzos had closed for the night. Florence is a remarkable city and staying at Casa Guidi has certainly heightened the experience.*

*Part of the apartment is open to the public by appointment on Monday, Wednesday and Friday afternoons, between April and November. It has some double glazing and partial air conditioning.*

Gallery    First floor

There are two bunks in the room above the shower room behind the double bedroom. This is reached by narrow spiral stairs.

# Piazza di Spagna

Rome

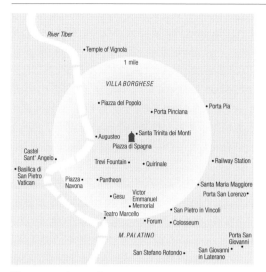

For up to 4 people
No private parking

All architects, and many artists, owe a debt to Rome, and we had long wanted a foothold there. So when the Keats-Shelley Memorial Association launched an appeal for funds to maintain 26 Piazza di Spagna, we asked whether there was a part of it that we could occupy in return for helping them. Happily there was, a flat on the third floor, now restored by us to its condition in about 1800 – spacious rooms with tiled floors and high, beamed ceilings painted in soft colours. The house itself was built around 1600, but owes its external appearence today to changes made by Francesco de Sanctis in 1724–5.

Our apartment is not the rooms in which Keats died in 1821 – those are on the floor below – but they are identical in form and layout, and are more in a condition he would recognise. Every tall shuttered window has a view unchanged almost since the days of the Grand Tour, and the sitting-room looks up the Spanish Steps – certainly the world's grandest and most sophisticated outdoor staircase – to the church of S. Trinita dei Monti at the top. At the front door is Bernini's fountain in the form of a stone boat sinking into the Piazza di Spagna. There is hardly any motor traffic, but instead the noises of humanity, some of them very unusual – for example when the steps are cleared by water-cannon at midnight, or when the horsedrawn cabs, which form a rank at the far end of the Piazza, arrive over the cobbles, seemingly at dawn and at a gallop.

The Steps were designed in 1721 by Francesco de Sanctis, who also designed this house to fit in with his plan. It was probably apartments from the first, in a part of the city long frequented by foreign and particularly English visitors. There can be few places in Rome available to their successors so central, so handsome, so famous or so unaltered as this.

Third floor

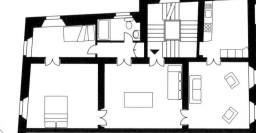

The apartment has double glazing and partial air conditioning. It does not have a lift.

# Sant' Antonio

Tivoli, near Rome

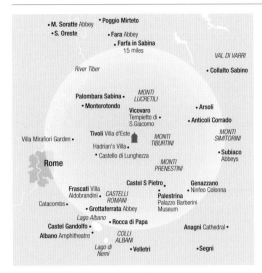

For up to 12 people
Open fire

Enclosed garden
Adjacent parking

Frederick Searle, who bought the old monastery of Sant' Antonio near Tivoli in 1878, first saw and fell in love with it when looking for a place from which to paint the great waterfall, across the ravine from the town. A visit today is equally one of enchantment: the little church at the top dedicated to the kindly Sant' Antonio of Padua; the simple rooms, each with a shuttered window opening on to the valley, the waterfall and Tivoli itself; the upper belvedere, giving a first full taste of what, with a few battered edges, can still be recognised as the 'loveliest view in the world'. Hints of a distant past appear in cells with mosaic floors, and in the kitchen, where on the inner wall is some 'opus reticulatum', a sign of Romans at work; but no moment is more thrilling than when, having passed through an arcaded loggia and down to the level of the fruitful, scented and beautiful terraced garden, an old door is opened in the house wall – a moment it would be unfair to spoil by describing in advance.

The truth is that the walls of a Roman villa, dated to about 60 BC and believed to have belonged to the poet Horace, survive up to the middle floor of the present house, itself begun in about 850 AD. Franciscan monks have lived here, and Popes. The final additions were made 'as late as the 17th century'. It was abandoned around 1870 and rescued by the Searles, who spent many years gently repairing it.

Sant' Antonio has descended to their great-great-grandson, who sought to give it a safe future. Knowing of our involvement with Keats' House in Rome, he asked us for help. With the greatest of pleasure, we are letting his house for him.

As if Sant' Antonio itself were not enough, at Tivoli you can visit the Villa d'Este, with its incomparable fountains, and Hadrian's Villa, the inspiration for many British garden buildings. Lazio, with its hills and lakes, its castles, gardens and wines, its relics of Rome and Etrusca, is one of the most beautiful and least-known regions of Italy.

From the logbook
*A room with a view is all very well – but a bathroom with a view; bliss.*

Upper floor

N

Stairs up to
Caretaker Flat

Sacristy
(not normally open)

Church
(not normally open)

Lower floor

Cellar

Cellar

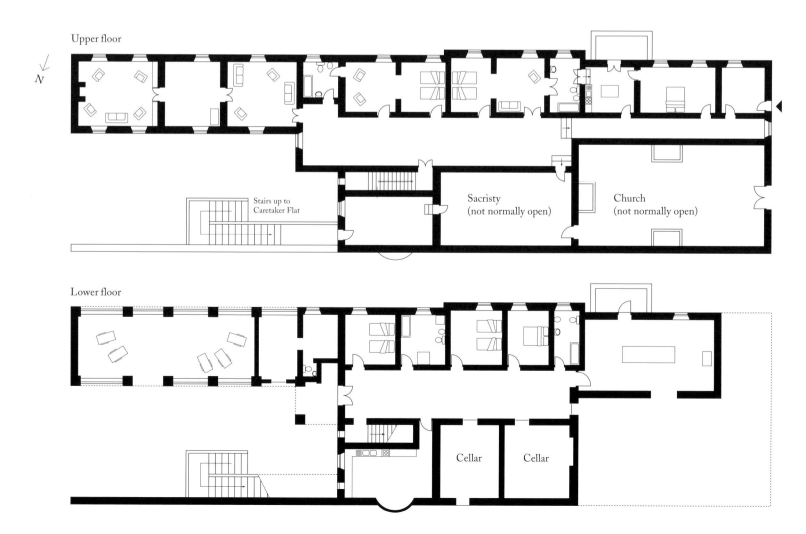

# Villa Saraceno

Finale, Vicenza

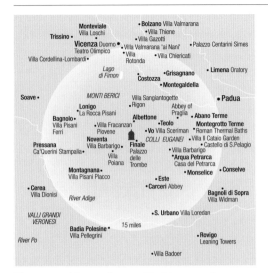

For up to 16 people

Open fire

Enclosed garden

Parking nearby

Dogs allowed

During the peaceful years in the middle of the sixteenth century, Italian culture displayed a desire to escape the bustle of the city that is strangely familiar to us today. The manner in which Andrea Palladio realised this ideal of a peaceful but cultured existence is one that had particular influence upon British architects. The fertile plain of the Veneto is sprinkled with archetypal Palladian villas like our own Villa Saraceno; some of these you can visit, but no other can you have to yourselves to taste this life of fulfilled recreation.

The villa was built c.1550 for Biagio Saraceno, a minor nobleman from Vicenza, to be both country retreat and working farm. Palladio's designs for the villa show a courtyard of colonnaded barns, although in the event only the main house was built. The adjoining buildings are mostly earlier in date, including the early Renaissance house in which most of you will sleep. The walled grounds provide a sense of seclusion, perfect for a quiet evening stroll in search of a ripe fig (and, if younger members of your party are so inclined, they make a splendid playing field).

After decades of neglect, we found all the buildings in a state of serious decay and their restoration was a lengthy and exciting process. Inside the main house, the original arrangement of entering through a grand sala has been recreated. The sala has huge granaries to explore above and is once again flanked by apartments of spacious rooms in which you will dine and sit. To our delight, beneath later layers of limewash we found lively frescoed friezes running around the sala's lofty cornices. There are more frescoes in the loggia and sitting room, which also has an open hearth for log fires on cooler evenings.

Just like the Renaissance noblemen for whom these villas were built, you can easily dip into urban sophistication if you wish. Our villa is little more than an hour from Venice and the towns of Padua and Vicenza are even closer, all full of architectural and modern day delights to discover. The plain rolls away on all sides of the villa, a country of poplars and canals and still mainly agricultural. How you choose to spend your days at the villa is up to you, but the chances are that you too will discover the truth of Palladio's explanation of the value of villa life.

From the logbook

*Late night walks by the cornfields with miniature fireflies lighting your way.*

*Magic evenings dining al fresco in the loggia.*

*Have felt no wish to leave the bounds of the Villa all week.*

*Parts of the villa are open to the public by appointment on Wednesday afternoons between April and October.*

Upper floor
Villa

Upper floor
Barchessa

Upper floor
Casa Vecchia

Granary

Lower floor
Piano Nobile
Villa

Lower floor
Barchessa

First floor
Casa Vecchia

Garden Room

Loggia (at
Ground Level)

Entrance floor
Casa Vecchia

N

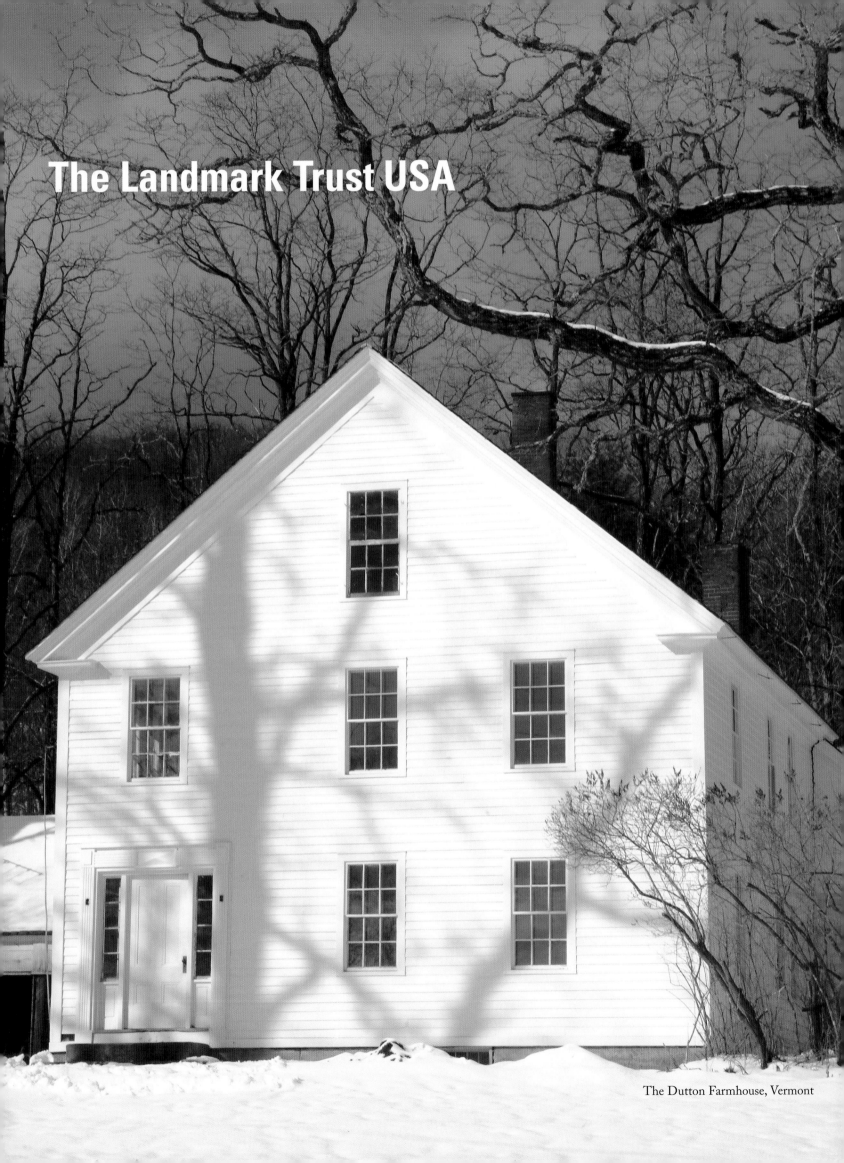

# The Landmark Trust USA

The Dutton Farmhouse, Vermont

# The Landmark Trust USA

The Landmark Trust USA is a tax-exempt non profit corporation established in 1991 in order to carry on preservation work in America according to the model established by the Landmark Trust. We are fully independent and responsible for our own projects and funding. Naulakha, Rudyard Kipling's Vermont home, was our first project.

The Landmark Trust USA considers education to be an essential part of our mission. We therefore make the process of conservative, traditional repair of our buildings an opportunity for fostering the building crafts through on-site training and workshops. At the Amos Brown House, our second project, we offered training sessions on the use of lime mortars.

The Trust also makes the completed sites available to local schools for special educational projects. Our 'Stories by Rudyard Kipling' program at Naulakha, for example, allows hundreds of school children every year to hear the *Just So Stories* where they were first told by Kipling to his daughter, Josephine.

One of our most exciting challenges is the 571 acre Scott Farm which abuts the 55 acre Naulakha property and which we have owned since 1995. Scott Farm has long been known for the quality of the apples from its 60-acre orchard. Landmark USA has broadened the appeal by adding over 60 varieties of heirloom apples and converting to low-spray, ecologically grown apples. We have also planted pears, plums, raspberries, gooseberries, grapes, and blueberries. We have restored the farm's Sugarhouse as a Landmark and will complete work on the Dutton Farmhouse in summer 2005.

Americans who would like to help the Landmark Trust USA to rescue neglected historic sites in the United States should contact our office in Vermont. There are many types of charitable donations with substantial tax benefits and our staff would be pleased to provide information and assistance. Your donation can help you minimise your tax burden while you support the conservation of historic resources for future generations.

**Landmark Trust USA, Inc.**
707 Kipling Road
Dummerston, Vermont, USA 05301
Telephone  802-254-6868
Fax  802-257-7783
Email  info@landmarktrustusa.org
Website  landmarktrustusa.org

**Board of Directors**
Mrs Marcia Hunker, Chair
Mr David Baxendale
Mr James Berkman
Mrs Mary Ann Clarkson
Mr Albert Hunker
Mr David Tansey

**Staff**
Mr David Tansey, Executive Director
Ms Kelly Carlin
Mr Peter Doubleday
Mr Ezekiel Goodband
Mr Scott Schadler

# Amos Brown House

Whitingham, Vermont

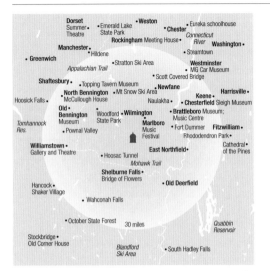

For up to 6 people
Gas stove

Garden and grounds
Adjacent parking

The Amos Brown House of 1802 is the oldest house in Whitingham, Vermont, less than a mile north of the Massachusetts border. While the area at the time must have been heavily forested, Amos Brown chose to build his home in brick which was fabricated on site. Designed with elements of the Federal style, the first style of the new American republic, the house also retained features that were common from the seventeenth century in New England.

The farm prospered and in the 1870s the house was expanded with the addition of a summer kitchen and pantry, porch, woodshed, chicken coop, barn and 4-seater outhouse, all of which remain virtually unchanged. Despite the fact that by this date Vermont had been nearly deforested for sheep farming, these additions were constructed in wood.

By the late nineteenth century the Amos Brown House began to decline, following the trend of agriculture in New England and in the 1930s farming at this site ceased. Soon afterwards this farm became the home of Carthusian monks, a contemplative order founded in France. For nearly 20 years the monks lived in shacks in the woods and held services and prepared meals in the house. An interesting reminder of their presence is a nearly complete set of the stations of the cross in ornate plaster relief with French inscriptions. These have been conserved and are now mounted in the woodshed.

Landmark USA acquired the property in 2000 from the local historical society who found the project beyond their means. Over two years we reversed the extensive deterioration and damage caused by neglect and ill-considered repairs. Visitors can now enjoy the humble beauty of the farmhouse and serenity of our 30 acres, far from highways and congestion.

Ground floor

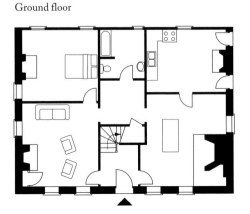

First floor

N ←

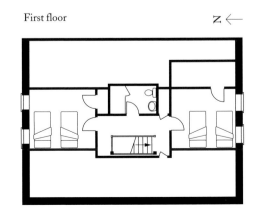

# The Dutton Farmhouse

Dummerston, Vermont

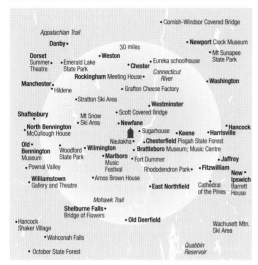

For up to 8 people
Gas stove
Extensive grounds

Adjacent parking
Access to clay tennis
court at Naulakha

The Dutton Farmhouse sits near the top of a hill and offers a broad vista eastward over the apple orchards of Scott Farm in the foreground and, beyond, the Connecticut River valley and Mount Monadnock 35 miles away. It lies near the centre of the Scott Farm with its 571 acres, four farmhouses and six barns, most generously given to Landmark USA by Fred Holbrook, a well known apple grower who wished to see his farm preserved.

The main house was built by Asa Dutton around 1840 in Greek Revival style and it sits proudly on a granite plinth. A mile down the road is another prominent farmhouse, built by Asa's brother. The brothers chose exceptionally beautiful sites and both featured large clapboarded barns; unfortunately the Asa Dutton barn burned down in the 1980s.

While investigating the structure of the Dutton Farmhouse, we discovered that the rear wing, although constructed of older components, was brought to the site later by Dutton. So, too,

were the very unusual Federal style decorations in the front parlour; the cornice with carved palm trees, stylised seashells and geometric elements came from an earlier house.

By the time we acquired this house, it had served as seasonal housing for apple pickers for over 30 years, lying empty and neglected most of the time. For a house of such high quality in such a beautiful location, this was indeed a strange fate but it had, at least, prevented extreme alterations.

The Dutton Farmhouse presents the finest of Vermont. Not a single house can be seen across a view of many miles, yet music festivals, ski areas, and beautiful towns are nearby. Visitors will, however, find the charm of exploring Scott Farm just as alluring as these attractions of civilization.

*The Dutton Farmhouse will be available for booking during 2005. Please contact the Booking Office for further information.*

Ground floor

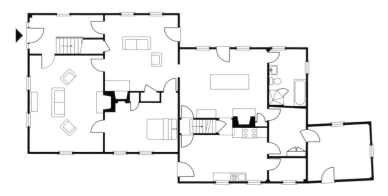

First floor

# Naulakha

Brattleboro, Vermont

For up to 8 people
Gas fire
Garden and grounds

Clay tennis court
Adjacent parking

In 1892 Rudyard Kipling and his new wife, Caroline, arrived in Vermont to stay with her family near Brattleboro. He was captivated by this new country and resolved to settle there permanently. He bought 11 acres of gently sloping pasture, and over the next winter supervised the building of a house, which he called Naulakha, the jewel beyond price.

The plans for Naulakha were drawn by H. R. Marshall, but Kipling saw its design as very much his own. He called it a ship, with his study at the bow. Here he could write in closely guarded privacy, with direct access to a verandah and flower garden. The main point of the house was the view, across woods and farmland to distant hills. Each room must enjoy this, making the house long and thin.

The Kiplings' ideal of a remote creative life in Vermont did not prosper. They left Naulakha in 1896 and circumstances and new directions made this an abandonment for good. By 1902, already living at Bateman's in Sussex, they were desperate to sell their American home, with much of its furniture. It was bought by a friend, Miss Cabot, and soon afterwards descended to the Holbrook family, from whom we bought it. In their gentle care the house kept a strong sense of its builder, and such small alterations as they made, we have now reversed. Many of the rooms thus remain exactly as Kipling knew them, including the study in which he wrote *The Jungle Books* and *Captains Courageous*.

Naulakha shows us a different Kipling to Bateman's. Here he was unharnessed by a romantic sense of history: each mark he made was his alone. And Vermont, with its forests and lakes, its quiet villages and unhurried life, summer music festivals and winter skiing, is as captivating as it was a century ago.

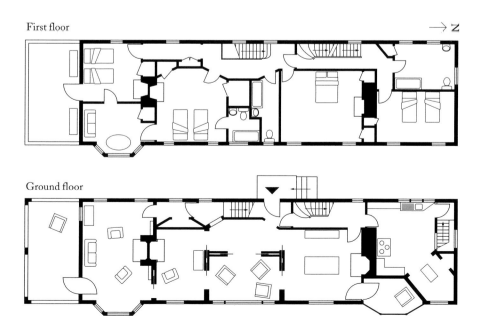

First floor

$\rightarrow$ N

Ground floor

# The Sugarhouse

Dummerston, Vermont

For up to 2 people
Gas stove
Extensive grounds

Adjacent parking
Access to clay tennis
court at Naulakha

Maple sugaring goes back many centuries in this part of North America. Native Americans were the first to recognise this gift of the forest and early settlers quickly learned the delight of 'Indian molasses', an early term for maple syrup. Benjamin Rush, a signer of the Declaration of Independence, wrote in a letter to Thomas Jefferson, 'The gift of the sugar maple trees is from a benevolent Providence'.

Our Sugarhouse dates from around 1900, although almost certainly it replaced another. It takes 40 gallons of sap to produce one gallon of maple syrup, a process which requires a great deal of boiling over large, intense fires. Sugarhouses were, therefore, prone to burning down, so that few early ones now survive. The very steep slate roof on our Sugarhouse is perhaps responsible for its survival by protecting it from flying sparks.

The eccentric shape of the building was perfectly suited to syrup making: long and narrow for the evaporator pan and tall with a monitor roof to allow the escape of steam. The room once used for the storage of sap buckets is now the bedroom while the bathroom is tucked into the woodshed.

Rudyard Kipling, who lived a short distance down the road, may well have been a customer of Scott Farm. He is known to have developed a taste for maple syrup on his pancakes and he did sign the Scott Farm guest book. Records reveal that Scott Farm was producing syrup by 1845 and, in the 1920s, it became one of the first to adopt mail-order marketing, soon shipping its syrup worldwide. 50 years later syrup production here ended and the Sugarhouse was converted to housing for farm workers.

The Sugarhouse is set back from the road up its own driveway flanked by stone walls.

From the logbook
*Everything you need, nothing you don't – the Sugarhouse was the perfect place to ring in the New Year.*

# People

In addition we gratefully acknowledge the voluntary help of numerous relatives and friends of the Landmark staff throughout the country.

# Acknowledgements

*Photographers*
*Front Cover* by John Miller
David Alexander, R Allenby-Pratt , Stuart Andrews, Archive Photography,
Constance Barrett, Clive Boursnell, Paul Barker, Derry Brabbs, Angus Bremner,
Country Life Picture Library/Paul Barker, Country Life Picture Library/
June Buck, M Campbell Cole, Martin Charles, Christopher Dalton,
James O Davies, R Emrett Bright, Rebekah Foxley, Paul Gummer,
P Douglas Hamilton, Janine Hall, Nicolette Hallett, Barry Hamilton,
Richard Hayman, Ross Hoddinott, Keith Hunter, Aldo Jacovelli, PS Kristensen,
Reg Lo-Vel, Peter Mauss/Esto, F Magonio, John Miller, James Morris,
Gary Moyse, Lee Pengelly, Geof Salt, Nigel Shuttleworth, Mr Christian Smith,
Caroline Stanford, Ian Sumner, David Tansey, Jonathan Thompson,
Tom Valentine, Matthew Weinreb, John Wilkie, Harry Williams, George Wright

We have credited those photographers whose work has been identified or
labelled and we apologise to those who have not been recorded as a result.

*Maps*
The location maps were drawn by Michael Robinson and other site maps by
Desmond Thomas.

Lundy Island map based on Ordnanace Survey mapping with the permission of
the Controller of Her Majesty's Office © Crown Copyright; Licence Number
MC100018629.

*Plans*
The plans were drawn by John Hewitt, based on original plans by
Michael Fleetwood.

© The Landmark Trust 2005
ISBN 0 9533124 4 5

The Handbook is as accurate as possible at the time of going to print.
We cannot be held liable for any inaccuracies that may arise.

Designed originally by Atelier Works
21st edition by Third Millenium Publishing
Reprographics by Asia Graphic Printing LTD, Hong Kong

Printed and bound in Slovenia by MKT Print d. d.
Printed on Primasilk 250gsm and 115gsm Bio-matt paper
(elementar chlorine free) from integrated and sustainable forestry
operations where controlled felling and replanting policies are practised.

Twenty-first Edition
Published May 2005

The Landmark Trust
Shottesbrooke
Maidenhead
Berkshire SL6 3SW
United Kingdom

Registered charity number 243312